W9-BRZ-638

Progressive Educators and the Catholic Church

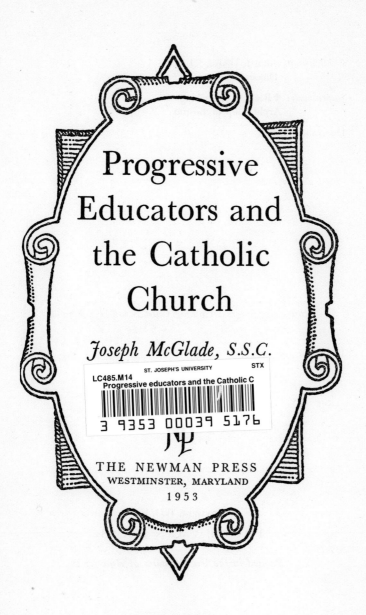

Progressive Educators and the Catholic Church

Joseph McGlade, S.S.C.

THE NEWMAN PRESS
WESTMINSTER, MARYLAND
1953

Nihil obstat: John J. Walsh, S.J.
              Diocesan Censor

Imprimatur: ✠ Richard J. Cushing
              Archbishop of Boston

December 31, 1952

Library of Congress Catalog Card Number: 53–5588

Foreword

Sir Arthur Quiller-Couch, for many years professor of English Literature at the University of Cambridge, made the following statement in one of his lectures:

> And here let me say that of all the books written in these hundred years there is perhaps none you can more profitably thumb and ponder than that volume of his [Newman's] in which, under the title of *The Idea of a University*, he collected nine discourses addressed to the Roman Catholics of Dublin with some lectures to the Catholic University there. It is fragmentary, because its themes were occasional. It has missed to be appraised at its true worth, partly no doubt by reason of the colour it derives from a religion still unpopular in England. But in fact it may be read without offence by the strictest Protestant; and the book is so wise—so eminently wise—as to deserve being bound by the young student of literature for a frontlet on his brow and a talisman on his writing wrist.[1]

The author of these words was speaking of literature and the practice of writing. Neither he nor anyone in his audience would deny, as he says in a later lecture, a prominent place to Newman among the masters of English prose. And yet because of the unfashionable-

[1] Sir Arthur Quiller-Couch, *On the Art of Writing* (New York: G. P. Putnam's Sons, 1916), p. 37.

ness of Catholicism in the England of that day, this masterpiece by Newman was not valued at its true worth.

The Idea of a University is indeed great writing. But it is more; it is great educational literature. On reading the words of Quiller-Couch, the thought comes to mind that a similar lack of due appreciation is evident today among educators throughout the United States, and for a reason similar to that alleged in the words we have just quoted. Catholic educational philosophy and the Catholic school system are not valued at their worth because, in educational circles, religion, and the Catholic religion in particular, is still unpopular. No further evidence is needed than that to be found in the many works on educational philosophy from the writers of most schools of thought.

In this book, we have presented such evidence from the representative books of the living leaders of progressive educational philosophy.

Acknowledgments

We wish to thank the following for graciously granting us permission to quote from their publications:

Appleton-Century-Crofts, Inc.—*Education and the Philosophy of Experimentalism* and *Education and Morals: An Experimental Philosophy of Education* by John L. Childs, and *The Educational Frontier*, edited by William Heard Kilpatrick;

The Dial Press, Inc.—*Education for Modern Man*, copyright by Sidney Hook;

Farrar, Straus & Young, Inc.—*The Education of Free Men: An Essay Toward a Philosophy of Education for Americans*, copyright by Horace M. Kallen;

G. P. Putnam's Sons—*On the Art of Writing*, copyright by Sir Arthur Quiller-Couch;

Harper & Brothers—*Ends and Means in Education: A Midcentury Appraisal* by Theodore Brameld, and *The Improvement of Practical Intelligence: The Central Task of Education* by Bruce R. Raup, George E. Axtelle, Kenneth D. Benne, and B. Othanel Smith;

The Macmillan Company—*Democracy as a Way of Life* and *Modern Educational Theories* by Boyd H. Bode, and *Education for a Changing Civilization* by William Heard Kilpatrick;

ACKNOWLEDGMENTS

National Catholic Welfare Conference—*The Catholic Priesthood: An Encyclical Letter* by Pope Pius XI;

Newson & Company—*Progressive Education at the Crossroads* by Boyd H. Bode;

World Book Company—*Patterns of Educational Philosophy: A Democratic Interpretation* by Theodore Brameld;

Yale University Press—*Education at the Crossroads* by Jacques Maritain.

Sincere thanks are due to Rev. Charles Donovan, S.J., Boston College School of Education, for unceasing encouragement and expert advice; to Rev. Edward Maguire, Columban Fathers, Brooklyn; and Rev. Bernard Rattigan, Department of Education, Catholic University, Washington, for wise suggestions. For checking the proofs, a debt of gratitude is owed to Rev. Donal O'Mahony and Rev. John Breakey of the editorial staff of the *Far East* magazine.

JOSEPH McGLADE

St. Columban's
Milton, Massachusetts
March 17, 1953

Contents

Foreword   v

Acknowledgments   vii

Introduction . . . Intellectual Justice   1

I.   Kilpatrick: Champion of Progressivism   9

II.   Bode: Exponent of Relativism   29

III.   Childs and Others: Philosophers of Experimentalism   54

IV.   Hook and Kallen: Spokesmen of Prejudice   92

V.   Brameld: Advocate of Reconstructionism   114

VI.   Democratic Application of Scientific Method   150

Bibliography   159

Index   161

𝔍𝔫𝔱𝔯𝔬𝔡𝔲𝔠𝔱𝔦𝔬𝔫 . . . INTELLECTUAL JUSTICE

/ Modern thinkers, except in totalitarian circles, consider that the individual is sacred, that merely being a man is worth a great deal.\ The ultimate basis of democracy is the estimation that you, as a man, are of as much value as any other. You, for example, may have qualities that I may lack; my talents may be of a different order from yours. You may live longer and make a greater impression on the world; I may have a shorter life with a lot less worry and a great deal more happiness. You may live on Park Avenue, I in the backwoods. But we are both men and what makes us human is of equal value. Such is the healthy truth enshrined in the American heart and effectively translated into the American way of life.

It is a truth that is accepted theoretically, at least, by every patriotic citizen; it is a truth for which America stands prepared to stake her all. The idea of democracy is held to be the ruling principle and supreme aim in the educational field. Yet, in the name of this great objective, a multitude of individuals seems to be thrust to one side with their thoughts, their ideas and ideals, their beliefs and values, their patriotism, their Americanism—all as of no great consequence and, indeed, sometimes as a great obstacle—and this, by a group of educators who profess for democracy an all-consuming zeal and devotion.

1

There are grounds for thinking that democracy as an aim and a means in the sphere of education is jettisoned when there is any question of Catholic Americans. They receive no consideration whatever or, if they are considered, their philosophy is rejected without due scientific examination and often, unfortunately, because of perverted or untrue interpretations of what that philosophy really is. And this rejection is being made in the name of the truth (for which these American Catholics are also prepared to stake their all) that the individual is sacred and free.

In the United States during the last fifty years, the currents of educational philosophy have been something of a swirling eddy. Not, it is true, that the year 1900 marked the definite starting point for contemporary theories or was even a decisive branching-off junction. None of the modern thinkers claims that he owes his thought entirely to himself or to our century. There are roots in the past, immediate or more remote. However, there can be little doubt that one particular school of philosophy has had a decisive influence on the educational scheme. John Dewey was its prophet; its name has changed according to the emphasis its leaders wished to give to some fundamental tenets. Most common among the names are progressivism, pragmatism and experimentalism.

Writers and thinkers of the progressive school have a noticeably uniform mode of procedure when it comes to the question of Catholic philosophy, Catholic educational theory and practice. So great is the power of this school in the educational world that it is worth while to investigate their credentials, examine their procedures, discuss their thought and evaluate their worth. It would be disastrous to trust the fate of the American way of life to unaccredited experts. The study we have undertaken aims at an evaluation of these thinkers. We have limited the discussion to a number of the outstanding leaders, men whose names are household words in educational circles. From that number we have omitted one to whom they all have given their allegiance—John Dewey. This omission is made, not because we think Dewey unimportant, but rather because we are more interested in those living leaders of the movement, many of whom are even now actively propagating these attitudes toward Catholic educational philosophy. A second limitation should be mentioned. We do not intend to examine all of the writings that have come from the pen of each author chosen. Our attention will be confined to one or two of the better-known and more representative works of each.

The problem we have set ourselves to investigate should provide an answer to the question of whether these philosophers have been true to their own declared principles of scientific investigation. Scientific method, tested thought, experimental procedure, sifting and evaluation of evidence, consideration of alternatives, honest and fair judgment of philosophies at variance with progressivism—such are the boasted techniques of the experimental school. They are indeed techniques which should lead to valid conclusions. We will judge these thinkers by their own standards. Our focus will be mainly on what they have to say about Catholic philosophy, Catholic education, Catholic beliefs. What they have said has not always been expressly said but rather implied and insinuated. Sometimes they have said nothing when they should have said something. Omission is often a scientific deficiency as real as the distortion of evidence. While we do not aim to give a complete critique of the philosophy of these pragmatist writers, we shall at times point out the inconsistencies to which some of their philosophic tenets lead or the invalid and unwarranted nature of some of their definitions. In fine, this book is not an exposition of Catholic educational philosophy, it is not a critical study of experimentalism; *it is a study of how men, professing loyalty to and complete confidence in the scientific method, have actually in practice applied that method when dealing with Catholicism.*

The educational techniques whose introduction in this century is the great contribution of the progressive school are in the main not opposed to Catholic thought. Hence, Catholic educators have seen fit to benefit by the introduction of such methods of teaching as are more adapted to modern social life and to democratic society. The Catholic Church is not afraid of any progress so long as it be truly scientific. But the philosophy of experimentalism, on the other hand, is fundamentally at variance with Catholic philosophy. The former is materialistic and is limited to what this world has to offer. The latter has a wider horizon; not only is it concerned with this world, but it is also built on the recognition of the existence of God, who is personally and practically interested in what goes on in this world. Experimentalism will have naught to do with absolute truths nor with supernaturalism. Catholicism believes that truths valid thousands of years ago are still valid today; it believes that man's conduct is to be guided by general principles which are still applicable in spite of the many changes that have taken place in social life and environment.

We do not expect to find agreement on our philosophical tenets, much less on our theological beliefs. We do expect not to be condemned unheard; we expect a fair trial in the philosophic domain, by jury as it were. We expect to be slandered—but not by educated men. We expect outsiders to be confused at times by the explanation of our beliefs and we are sure that they will not always understand, but we expect the scholarly outsider to try honestly to see our side of the question. Experience teaches us that discussions can descend at times to the purely emotional level. We realize that intellectual differences can breed bigotry on both sides, for thinkers of all schools are but human, with likes and dislikes, with attitudes and prejudices which it is not always easy to control. But we expect that, in circles where the scientific method is professedly held in such high esteem, there will be evidence of objectivity in dealing with Catholicism. Of this we have found very little in the literature of the progressives. Thus, we hope that this brief study will suggest to the reader the need for a retrial before accepting conclusions hostile to Catholicism. We cannot consider the whole case here, but simply direct attention to the uncritical condemnation of Catholic educational thought and practice by well-known American educators.

The education of American youth, as of all youth, is a matter of supreme importance because of the present world situation. To be alive today means to be caught in what looks like a maelstrom of conflicting social forces and ideologies, carrying a whirling international world to the brink of disaster. To many, indeed, that disaster seems so imminent as to destroy all hope of escape. Even the more optimistic and prudent gaze with misgivings at the veil which hangs over the events to be disclosed by the unfolding of the next fifty years. The history of the last half-century has revealed to all of us some of the most brutal examples of inhumanity of which humans could be capable; for evidence, we need only point to death-camps like Dachau and Buchenwald. It is true, however, that the half-known history of that era reveals another aspect that redounds to the great credit of modern man. Witness the amazing advance of technology and science! Men of genius have been able to wrest from nature many long-hidden secrets; they have harnessed its powers and gained knowledge which they have applied in all fields to make life fuller and happier. The new advances in communication and transportation have made our world international in a way that was never before envisaged. No part of the earth is now remote, no nation or people is greatly removed from the influence of Western civilization, no war fails to have its effect everywhere. We live in an era in which mankind should be able to achieve the greatest prosperity, peace and happiness. Yet we still see millions of refugees on the face of the earth, and millions in slave camps and enforced labor gangs; we see the powerful dominating the weak and the lifeblood of many nations being drained away.

In the conflict that has now developed, two powers have emerged in opposing camps. Politically and nationally, they are the United States and Russia. No one, however, can analyze the situation without seeing that the cause lies deeper than national interests and political power. A gauntlet has been thrown down—the challenge of one ideology to another, of communism to democracy. Democracy is a fuzzy term that receives many interpretations. Suffice it to say here that its general meaning is the way of life which the writers of the American Constitution tried to establish and guarantee. Communism means slavery to the state. Observers declare that communism owes its tremendous success in Russia to the enthusiasm of its youth. Americans claim that the hope of the future is in the youth of the land. What youth believes, what they aim for, the values they cherish, the lines of conduct they follow, are all of supreme importance. Small wonder then that educators in the United States have wished to build for democracy, have aimed at guaranteeing freedom rather than slavery, have declared that the individual is sacred because he is a human person.

We believe that the 112,000 Catholic schools with their 3,500,000 American pupils are in the vanguard of that struggle for Christian democracy. We wince when we read the bland statement that the Church and its leaders are as bad as, if not worse than, any of the dictators. We are provoked when we learn that people believe that a good Catholic cannot be a good American. We are shocked when we find that our centuries-old system of thought is dismissed in a patronizing sentence or two. We are moved to give voice when we see that educational institutions throughout the land are greatly influenced by the teachings of educational leaders who propagate such views of Catholicism. The one purpose of this study is to call attention to the pattern of misrepresentation and unscholarliness to be found in the writings of prominent progressive educators when they discuss Catholic thought and belief. We do not quote, except rarely, from Catholic sources. We have tried to be fair to the thought of the writers studied. We hope that we have proceeded in a scientific and objective way. We leave the rest to the fair-minded reader.

Chapter One . . . KILPATRICK: CHAMPION OF PROGRESSIVISM

William Heard Kilpatrick can now look back on a long life spent in the educational field. As disciple and co-partner of John Dewey, he was in the vanguard of the progressive movement. During his many years at Teachers College, Columbia University, he did much to spread the influence of Dewey. Nor was he limited by the confines of one college; his extensive writings carried his thought to educators all over the country. It seems fitting, then, to begin our study with some of Kilpatrick's writings. In calling him an early leader, we wish in no way to question his continued standing in the experimentalist school. We have chosen three lectures, delivered in 1926 at Rutgers University, as a good introduction to the exposition of the philosophy considered in the chapters to follow.[1] In these lectures, Kilpatrick proposed briefly the main tenets of progressivism. Later we will look at an important work of collaboration of which he was editor.

1

The most important idea Kilpatrick wished to emphasize concerning modern society was that of change. The common man can easily note, accurately

[1] William Heard Kilpatrick, *Education for a Changing Civilization* (New York: The Macmillan Company, 1927).

9

enough, the tremendous difference there is between the world of the twentieth century and the world of an earlier era. According to our author, the explanation of such almost headlong progress is to be found in the concept of tested thought.[2] People no longer accepted ideas and statements as truth on the mere authority of leaders; they wanted to test for themselves, to find out the reason why, to sift evidence. In the sphere of science and technology, such a procedure is invaluable; yet we learn that it was not confined to these spheres. The changed mental outlook—one of three distinctive trends noted by our author in modern life [3]—considered nothing too sacred to be exempt from scientific scrutiny.

The second important trend of twentieth century society is its industrialism. This spelled a change from a certain independence, in economic matters, for the individual and family to a complete interdependence which is best exemplified in our huge industrial cities. Developments in means of transportation, in methods of production and in world-shaking weapons of war have proved the vivid truth of Kilpatrick's vision.

Democracy is the third trend underscored by our author. He was aware, of course, that it does not answer so well as the other two to the procedure of tested thought. For him "democracy is essentially life, ethical life." [4] In spite of the many difficulties which

[2] *Ibid.*, pp. 9 ff.
[3] *Ibid.*, pp. 16–29.
[4] *Ibid.*, p. 28.

industrialism places in the way of true democracy, the democratic way seems to be the "only program that can command abiding support." [5] Hand in hand with the spread of democracy went a corresponding wane in authoritarianism. Kilpatrick defined this term as an unquestioning acceptance of tradition without any reason for accepting it.[6] The root of the word is the same as for "authority," but the author warned against any confusion of the two ideas.[7] Authority cannot be external; presumably, if it is, we have authoritarianism. The internal authority of "how it works when tried" [8] is alone acceptable.

In the brief express treatment of this question and in many implications throughout the book, Kilpatrick set forth ideas which loom large in all expositions of progressive philosophy in succeeding years. We agree with his condemnation of the acceptance, without personal testing, of propositions which are subject to personal testing. But we certainly cannot agree that personal testing is the only valid source of truth. We certainly cannot agree that external authority, that is, the acceptance of the findings of individuals and groups whose knowledge and sincerity can be trusted, may be dispensed with in the twentieth century. It is true that a great deal of education in the past was carried out in an authoritarian way; it is also true that the content of that education was largely what we

[5] *Ibid.*, p. 29.
[6] *Ibid.*, p. 30.
[7] *Ibid.*, p. 29.
[8] *Ibid.*, p. 82.

call tradition. Kilpatrick would then have us believe that truths thus handed down must be rejected because the mode of acceptance was not that of tested truth. Obviously, they should be rejected only when they are found not to be truths. Kilpatrick implied that, because they were handed down, they were not truths; he did no more, he failed to disprove them. Here is a colossal example of apriorism, quite the opposite of the method of tested truth.

The outlook of the individual and society changed on moral questions, although, according to our author, "authoritarian morality had an apparent simplicity about it that inherent morals seem to lack." [9] Much could be said on these words, but it is sufficient to note the use of the term "inherent." What does it mean? As far as we can judge, inherent morals are such as rest on internal authority. In other words, it is up to the individual to judge of the goodness and badness of actions and to act accordingly rather than be guided by any answers from outside sources. Such a principle seems to grant infallibility to the conscience of each individual; if not, then it seems to matter little what people do so long as they can satisfy themselves by their own answers to the moral questions they inevitably have to face.

Among the changes in moral outlook, Kilpatrick believed the questioning attitude of youth to be very significant. No longer is it sufficient to say that a particular action is forbidden; young people want to

[9] *Ibid.*, p. 36.

know why. Through the illustrations given, Kilpatrick implied that no one told youth why or else they gave unsatisfactory reasons; consequently, youth went and did what was formerly forbidden. The conclusion he would have us draw is that the forbidden actions could not have been wrong because no one told youth why they were wrong. Hence, society is no longer caught in the stagnation of absolute moral standards. Let us, however, assume this much-lauded questioning attitude and ask why young people are right in their rejection of older ideas of right and wrong. If former prohibitions were based on unreasonable grounds, then praised be youth for its rejection of such standards. If, on the other hand, youth asked the question "Why?" and went off without waiting for an answer or investigating the answer given, then the unreasonableness lay with youth.

Kilpatrick himself foresees danger in the new morality he proposes. He feels obliged to make some apology for it.

> Of course the danger is that the shift will be only *from* external authority and not *to* a basis of internal authority. In plainer words, the danger is that for a while at least no authority at all will obtain, that there will be an interval of moral chaos.[10]

Our author's prophetic vision may have partly failed him in this instance; he did not see how long would be

[10] *Ibid.*, p. 37.

13

that "interval" of moral chaos caused by the move from external authority. He would most probably not admit that such moral chaos still rules where individuals are guided by their own internal authority. Certainly, after pointing out the obvious danger of his ethical individualism, Kilpatrick concludes in a burst of wishful thinking.

> Authoritarianism wanes but, granted wise enough leadership, the outlook for the future is for finer and better morals.[11]

We pause to ask whether that wise leadership is not a reintroduction of external authority, of authoritarianism.

The trends noted by our author in the development of social life brought the spotlight of his investigation on one important social factor—change.[12] We can readily agree that this is an important factor. We can agree, too, that the accelerated change in our century has made it very important to give more attention to this phenomenon. We do not, however, believe that change is the basis on which philosophy must be built. Aristotle, we are informed, gave a measure of recognition to the concept of change—limited, orderly change. Furthermore, Kilpatrick tells us, his essential assumptions were so subtly indoctrinated that today we find ourselves committed to them especially when we are expressing exact thought. (We might recall

[11] *Ibid.*, p. 38.
[12] *Ibid.*, p. 41.

that exact thought is what *we* expect from both philosophy and science.) But then Darwin came and thereafter anything might happen.

> There is no telling what may happen. In James's startling words, the lid is thus taken off the universe. The future is yet to be determined. No prior formulation will certainly hold in any realm. All old certainties are questioned.[13]

Before proposing some of the deficiencies manifested in Kilpatrick's exaggerated emphasis on change, we ask leave to digress from the field of philosophy proper and make a suggestion from the field of semantics. *To question* has several meanings in common use; one of these is to ask, to seek for information. Another meaning is *to doubt*. We are of the opinion that scientific method signifies the way of exact investigation. The questioning attitude which this implies is the great merit of the scientific method. Such an attitude, however, can be part of our scientific apparatus without committing us to the philosophy of doubt. Progressive thinkers, on the other hand, although they disclaim a real philosophy of doubt, seem always to give this meaning to the word we are discussing. The suggestion we would make is that readers remain always conscious of this progressive practice. The reason for this advice is that, especially in the discussion of moral truths, to adopt the questioning attitude is immediate proof to progressives that those moral propositions are untrue.

[13] *Ibid.*, p. 44.

Accelerated change in society has produced a phenomenon that modern sociologists designate as social lag. Kilpatrick signalized an important example of this in the labor-capital question (an instance that has since, to some extent, been corrected).[14] Though the just and fair conditions in this field were known, the necessary social machinery was not set up for the solution of difficulties. Even today, twenty-six years later, we are far from having reached the complete answer. History reveals other glaring examples which Kilpatrick did not mention. Take, for instance, the institution of slavery; its belated abolition typified social lag. There is also the degraded status of women, even today, in many countries that have a good measure of civilization.

Kilpatrick found an explanation for this lag in the fact that we did not keep our moral and intellectual life abreast of the changes that took place in material and technological spheres.[15] Social lag is not something to be defended; the examples given show clearly that it is to be deplored and abolished as quickly as possible. Yet this factor should not lead to the conclusion that our author seems to indicate, that unlimited (and possibly disorderly) change is the key to the philosophic difficulty. By way of illustrating his thesis, he mentioned that "movement itself may bring stability."[16] A spinning top or a moving bicycle will

14 *Ibid.*, p. 46.
15 *Ibid.*, p. 47.
16 *Ibid.*

stay upright only as long as they are kept in motion. Such examples do not strengthen Kilpatrick's criticism of Aristotle's outlook on change. Recall that our author declared Aristotle to hold that "change so conceived is orderly, decent, bounded, predictable." [17] With the lid off the universe, the implication seemed to be that there was no limit to change. Kilpatrick himself, however, says no more than that there is no limit to the rate of change—an entirely different concept. In the illustrations he gave, change is orderly and limited and is not an end in itself but the means of producing the desired stability (a sort of fixity). If we try to get beyond the limits of change that keeps a bicycle upright—this we can do by trying to change suddenly the direction of the motion—we shall find that such change, not being orderly, ends in mild disaster. Similarly, it is only when the motion of a top is in a certain direction and beyond a certain rate that the top remains upright. The sphere of astronomy offers a more striking example if our author cared to take it. Change, in the example of stellar movements, is but a more complicated instance of stability and motion. Such change is always within limits, is always orderly. If the lid were taken off in that sphere, there certainly would be no telling what might happen.

Kilpatrick cites Aristotle's explanation of change from potentiality to actuality as exemplified in the development of the oak from acorn, acorn from oak

[17] *Ibid.*, p. 42.

in endless series.[18] Whatever may be our author's reflections on this example of change, it is without doubt one that can be verified by means of experimental procedure. Furthermore, no scientist has yet produced evidence to show that an acorn ever developed into anything but an oak tree or that an oak produced some other type of seed than an acorn.

Perhaps it is not quite just to base our objections to Kilpatrick's doctrine of change on examples taken from another field and chosen by the author merely as figures. Illustrations of this kind should not be pushed too far since they were not meant to typify, point for point, the change that is so noticeable in social life. We do not believe that motion as an example of change in the sphere of either physics or astronomy is equivalent to change in the social life of humans. We must then agree with Kilpatrick in his implied criticism of Aristotle to the effect that change is not always predictable, especially in social trends that sometimes depend on unpredictable humans. Yet our author himself wanted to find "an analogous 'moving equilibrium' for our social affairs." [19] It seems that the analogy he found goes no further than the evidence of stability in the midst of change. Such evidence indicates that there is as much stability as change and that change which disrupts stability is no asset to social life.

The philosophy thus championed by Kilpatrick

[18] *Ibid.*, p. 42.
[19] *Ibid.*, p. 47.

brought consequences in the educational field. The main changes demanded of the modern school should be "an intelligent moralization of the adaptive *why* of conduct always underlying its *what;* second, methods of attack upon unsolved social problems; and, third, strong moral characters with broad-view social outlook and attitudes." [20] It should be noticed that the author placed his emphasis mainly on the moral sphere though morals is not the specific field of educators as such. Learning, we are informed, is "to acquire a way of behaving." [21] This definition is an unwarranted limiting of the notion of learning. While our external conduct will be governed by our internal attitudes and ways of thinking, there is no reason why learning must always lead to action.

Further complications arise from the pragmatist outlook on learning. The teacher, Kilpatrick has said, has responsibility in giving direction to learners. How can the teacher know whether he is acting wisely or not? "The test is what is learned." [22] In the years of schooling, the teacher has some opportunity of knowing what was learned since the pupils will have to make decisions and perform actions. But the future is unknown, according to experimental philosophy; we cannot impose our solutions on coming generations. Teachers will very often have ceased to teach by the time their pupils have given evidence of what they

[20] *Ibid.*, p. 94.
[21] *Ibid.*, p. 97.
[22] *Ibid.*, p. 129.

19

have learned. Hence, it is going to be extremely unfortunate for those people if they have not learned. Their failure will be of no advantage to the present generation of teachers and pupils; different times will have brought different problems requiring new solutions.[23]

Actually, Kilpatrick found it impossible to commit himself consistently to his ideas of change. He recognized that it is not possible to make "the school a complete reproduction in miniature of the social order." [24] He saw that we must know the goal if we are to teach consistently; he realized that some standards must be adopted. Even in such a simple matter of school practice as giving the children movable chairs instead of fixed desks in straight rows, our author has not been consistent.[25] Children have never ceased to go to the movies and be interested in them although the seats are fixed in straight rows and there is barely room even for children to stretch their legs.

Some points mentioned by Kilpatrick receive more attention from the later leaders and consequently we shall devote more space to them in later chapters. It may be noted here, however, that Kilpatrick, while recognizing the close relationship between education and religion, sees fit to dismiss in a few words the tenets of religion and the principles of morality.[26] The

[23] *Ibid.*, p. 85.
[24] William Heard Kilpatrick, editor, *The Educational Frontier* (Used by permission of Appleton-Century-Crofts, Inc.), p. 21.
[25] Kilpatrick, *Education for a Changing Civilization*, p. 90.
[26] *Ibid.*, p. 78.

necessity of handing on the culture of the group in its moral, religious, social and political aspects is held to be important: but call that culture tradition and then he rejects it.[27] Childhood must not wrongly be regarded as the vestibule of life; it is "an integral room in the house of life. . . ."[28] Kilpatrick's doctrine seems to make the house of life a house without rooms, no dividing walls, no rooms whose doors can be closed. Life is not like that; there are times when some doors will be locked; there are some people to whom all our doors are locked; there are few people to whom all our doors are unlocked, wide open. A philosophy should not be too abstracted from reality.

2

William Kilpatrick acted as editor for a yearbook on the philosophy of education which the National Society of College Teachers of Education requested.[29] It was admirably suited to express the stand of the progressive school, not only because of the material offered but also because so many of the leaders of that school took part in the collaboration. It is particularly suited to our purpose because in subsequent chapters we deal with later writings by most of these authors. In the yearbook, the chapters of the various authors clearly contain the seeds of thought that grew into the works they have issued more recently.

Professor Kilpatrick contributed two chapters to

[27] *Ibid.*, pp. 56–57.
[28] *Ibid.*, p. 76.
[29] *The Educational Frontier.*

this yearbook, one on adult education and the other on professional education. In these chapters we find statements that would seem to contradict the views of other progressives on similar matters. For example, Kilpatrick declared that procedures and techniques should always be subordinate to the general aims of life and education.[30] It will be worth recalling this when we see progressives claiming their method as a philosophy, the authority of method replacing the authority of creed, as they say. Bode especially considered that traditional education was aristocratic; Kilpatrick had something to say about background. With regard to teachers:

> The better cultural background, in spite of a certain apparent undemocratic aspect, cannot be disregarded.[31]

Kilpatrick seems to have felt that he must apologize at least a little for demanding "better cultural background" for teachers. The common man comes much to the fore in recent writings, and "common consents" (that is, by the majority) are to be the important measure of values. Look at the possibilities that the editor of *The Educational Frontier* saw in trusting to the majority. Speaking of the disadvantages of advertising (now immeasurably increased because of television), he stated:

[30] *Ibid.*, p. 261.
[31] *Ibid.*, p. 264.

> On the bad side will be the temptation to appeal
> to the lower ideals and taste of the majority
> rather than pursue the highest attainable ideals.[32]

It would seem then that Kilpatrick believed that the
majority could be fairly easily weaned away from
the highest possible ideals.

The need for self-criticism was evident to our
author. He advocated the "conscious definite effort to
see our inconsistencies. . . ."[33] We would like to
point out one inconsistency he must have missed in his
effort. He gave a definition of true individuality, a
quality to be highly valued.

> To hold out against others after thought and
> because thought demands it—this is true indi-
> viduality.[34]

On the merely philosophical and sociological plane,
Kilpatrick should have seen that that is precisely what
Catholic educators have done, but he and writers of
his school consider such a genuinely thoughtful stand
mere obscurantism when it is taken to defend traditional truth and morality.

> In moral and religious affairs divine revelation
> through book and church was the one sole and
> sufficient foundation.[35]

Strangely enough, this declaration by Kilpatrick is
almost accurate. Unfortunately, he does not mean the

[32] *Ibid.*, p. 138.
[33] *Ibid.*, p. 260.
[34] *Ibid.*, p. 262.
[35] *Ibid.*, p. 122.

same thing as we do by the term "divine revelation." For him, its basis was superstition; for us, the philosophic motivation for believing a revelation to be divine (which we must be sure of before we believe the revelation) is supplied by reasoned thought.

In one chapter whose co-authors were Dewey and Childs, we find a refreshingly modest disclaimer to the effect that the progressives do not pretend to offer *the* philosophy of education; in fact, they do not believe "there is any such thing." [36] Nevertheless, the experimental way is claimed by them as the only one compatible with the American way of life.[37] It must be remembered that for the experimentalist his method is the true means of answering all the problems of life. We are thus led to suspect that they really do claim to possess *the* philosophy of education. To a great extent, experimental thought was something new although its proponents realized that there was tested thought even in traditional times. It is claimed as the key to modern problems; it is, we are led to believe, one of the blessings that has evolved from our dynamic and changing civilization. This school of philosophy has from its beginning assumed a role of leadership in the educational field. But it cannot stand simply on the fact that it is new. Nor is it sufficient that the older philosophies showed themselves unable or unwilling to cope with problems in the past (even if this general statement could be proved). There must be

[36] *Ibid.*, p. 287.
[37] *Ibid.*, p. 317.

some positive contribution, not only in the matter of teaching techniques but on the plane of philosophy. The sweeping wave of the experimentalist hand or the supercilious raising of the progressive eyebrow may make an impression; they are none the less insufficient grounds for rejecting established moral truths.

The leaders who contributed to this work declared that progressive thought is positive; they are not content with vague generalizations. Vital matters must not be left to chance in the education of the young; [38] "beliefs, convictions, ideals, common consents, and mutual understandings" are necessary;[39] such being the case, the teacher must bring some order into his own mind on moral questions.[40] Catholics concur completely with these principles; we would, however, draw attention to the fact that, if these principles are not vague generalizations, they demand some fixity of standards. If they are not based on some such standards, we must believe that progressive thought is lost in a fog of verbiage. Catholic educators have made such principles their rule for action; they have always been able to base their way of life on reasonable grounds.

A major claim revealed in *The Educational Frontier*, as in all succeeding statements of this philosophy, is that of liberating education and thought from enslave-

[38] *Ibid.*, p. 261.
[39] *Ibid.*, p. 75.
[40] *Ibid.*, p. 125.

ment to superstition and supernatural authoritarianism. It would indeed be idle to deny that there was dictatorial procedure in traditional schools; it would be equally idle to deny that there is authoritarianism in public and progressive schools today. Teachers and administrators are not perfect characters. Even though educators as a group may be accorded a sort of moral personality, the cohesion that exists among them is not sufficient to nullify their individual imperfections. Experimentalists believe that criticism by the group will guarantee sound leadership and wise decisions (and the authors even conceded that occasionally such leadership would be offered by one man).[41] While recognizing the value of group decisions, we should not lose sight of the fact that neither infallibility nor unfaltering wisdom is conferred by a mere plurality of heads. Yet, the work under discussion put only one limit on educators, and that a very subjective one.

> There is but one limit to the power of an organized body of educators; that is the limit inherent in its own sense that it represents the people.[42]

Such a statement was probably made in the sincerity of high purpose. Taken objectively, it contains more arrogance than any of the alleged dictatorial claims of the Catholic Church. Educators are not elected by the people (even political representatives of the people

[41] *Ibid.*, p. 115.
[42] *Ibid.*

26

are, when duly elected, limited by more than their own sense of responsibility); educators represent the people only in the sense that they hold an important social position. The people might conceivably be better pleased if some educators spent their time and influence in a different sphere. Educators have taken to themselves a power to which they will raise no limit but their own subjective sense that they are doing the right thing for education. As to religious truths, the best treatment these men were prepared to concede was "a certain measure of benevolent protection." [43] This benevolence had a strange flavor. The churches, the authors maintained, were doing propaganda work on the side and at best their activity was on a level with that of study groups.[44] At worst, however, this activity was on the same level as the totalitarian propaganda machines.

Would it be reactionary on our part to appeal to a traditional document on behalf of at least one important religious truth? In the minds and hearts of the American people, one historical figure remains endeared in a lasting way—Abraham Lincoln. His Gettysburg address, brief though it be, can be repeated year after year and stir great sentiments and wonderful ideals. When the script of that address was given to him, he made one revision; he inserted the words "under God." If faced with the choice of following the progressive's rejection or Lincoln's

[43] *Ibid.*, p. 14.
[44] *Ibid.*, p. 140.

acceptance of God, the Americans who would follow Lincoln would be not merely sentimental but reasonable. Neither the repetition of the word "change" like some magical incantation, nor the appeal to subjective feeling under the name of tested thought, nor the appeal to the opinion of a group of educators guided only by their sense of what is right can discredit the common man's belief in God. The philosophers of experimentalism will have to come up with something more philosophical if they wish to undergird their infidelity. As it is, the wide influence that these men have had in precisely the areas we have been discussing here is a clear example of a type of authoritarianism: these men have "names" and they have numbers, and their categorical decrees are accepted unquestioningly by docile teachers and professors of education the country over.

Chapter Two . . . BODE: EXPONENT OF RELATIVISM

A very distressed but sincere voice has rung out on behalf of progressivism from the halls of Ohio State University. Professor Bode sees many dangers inside the progressive school itself. There are growths which wrongly claim to be progressive, exaggerations of methods introduced by Dewey's philosophy; there seems to be an unawareness of the necessity for an underlying philosophy. If progressivism and democracy are to mean anything they must mean a way of life. Bode's writings leave no doubt that their author is in deadly earnest in his quest for a sound philosophic basis for progressivism. He refers to weaknesses seldom noticed by followers of Dewey; for example, unbalanced devotion to the scientific method, the excesses of child-centeredness, the danger of substituting a new absolutism in place of the rejected traditionalism, the lack of aim in American education. In his philosophy for the survival of democracy, our author very definitely sweeps away all former basic beliefs and values. Nevertheless, in his own proposals he shows a good deal of doubt and vagueness. For instance, he considers the question of how the school is to build up the appropriate basic beliefs and rid the child of such attitudes as he may bring with him to school. He finds no definite answer to this question.

Perhaps there is no completely satisfactory answer to this question, but we must do the best we can.[1]

How vague this best is going to be is somewhat indicated by his declarations that democratic education is an adventure in *faith*,[2] that his conclusions are backed by a faith [3] that they will lead to a democratic way of life (which, however, he cannot guarantee). Such faith must not be belittled, if we follow Bode's thought; after all, it is linked with the idea of democracy, an idea, mark you, which the author tells us cannot be defined. If we, on the other hand, introduce a faith that is coupled with religion, we are accused of introducing superstition to young minds. Religion must be sedulously barred from the schools.[4]

In Bode's thought the idea of democracy is of paramount importance. For him it is no mere political arrangement for arriving at decisions through the vote of the greatest number. It should be a way of life.

In other words, it provides a comprehensive plan for the organization of both individual and collective conduct, which is essentially what is meant when we speak of a *way of life*.[5]

[1] Boyd H. Bode, *Democracy as a Way of Life* (New York: The Macmillan Company, 1948), p. 77.

[2] *Ibid.*, p. 113.

[3] *Ibid.*, p. 104.

[4] Boyd H. Bode, *Modern Educational Theories* (New York: The Macmillan Company, 1927), p. 67.

[5] Bode, *Democracy as a Way of Life*, p. 7.

The concept has undergone some changes since the Declaration of Independence and the drawing up of the Constitution of the United States. The early local independence of American communities represented a sort of dictatorship over the individual who elected to stay in a particular community. The standards of conduct were preserved by non-legal sanctions. If the individual disliked the limitations imposed on his freedom, he could, it is true, move elsewhere. Today, on the other hand, democracy puts great emphasis on the sacredness of the individual and this development of the concept has brought wider implications. Bode points out that the earlier practice suited the times;[6] he does not deny that the Founding Fathers did establish democracy. This concession can be turned against him, however. As he says, we have no right to interpret historical social factors in the light of modern attitudes and ideals. Thus, even were we to grant to Bode that traditional education and the Church (we mean the Catholic Church) formerly used methods of teaching which would not be approved now, such methods should not be judged solely in the light of modern conditions. Nowhere do the protagonists of progressivism even consider the possibility that perhaps older types of teaching were suited to the times. Obligations and duties were more readily acknowledged (even Bode lays obligations and duties on the democratic man [7]); deceit was not so widespread;

[6] *Ibid.*, p. 28.
[7] *Ibid.*, p. 80.

literacy was of no great avail when books were not easily procurable; opportunities for an improved social situation were not so numerous because no television engineers, auto mechanics, aeronautic experts, atomic scientists, advertising specialists and supersalesmen were needed. Such historical perspective does not enter into their criticism. The Church is regularly condemned for not being ahead of the times.

Bode has very definite ideas on the consequences of adopting a particular way of life. It must be the guiding star of all conduct and permeate all that a person does. There can be no compromise although there may be tolerance of those who differ.[8] In this matter we are in complete agreement with the author. Bode then meets a difficulty which his readers would certainly propose; he himself has the honesty and courage to bring it out into the open.[9] If democracy is to be a way of life, must it then be a sort of dictatorship? Compromise on principles is not possible; otherwise the way of life ceases to be that comprehensive plan for conduct which should be its essence. The whole structure of Bode's work seems to stand or fall on the solution of the proposed difficulty. He is satisfied with his answer to the problem. We think and hope to show that he has given an answer that is no solution.

Just as surely as, in Bode's mind, traditional education and absolute standards or truths fostered aris-

[8] *Ibid.*, p. 10.
[9] *Ibid.*, p. 16.

tocracy, so does democracy spell the era of the common man. We stand with Bode in his championship of the common man, but we think that he has committed the fault of forgetting many of the most common things about the common man. One such thing is human nature; another is the truth that the common man has always existed no matter what may have been the social attitudes, conventions and ideals. If he existed in a state of slavery or quasi-servitude, we maintain that because of his human nature, his individual personality, he had a right to a way of life befitting a human and no one could take that right away from him. Bode thinks he had no such right. Perhaps the casual reader would immediately raise indignant objection to this interpretation of our author's thought. Surely nothing could be farther away from Bode's mind. But what else can we conclude when he tells us that experience and experience alone provides principles of conduct?

> . . . social and ethical and esthetic principles are neither handed to him [man] ready made nor so imbedded in the structure of things that he need but look in order to discover them.[10]

It would be wrong, in Bode's thought, to appeal to human nature as basis for such inalienable rights as we enjoy in a democracy.[11] They are created out of

[10] Boyd H. Bode, *Progressive Education at the Crossroads* (New York: Newson and Company, 1938), p. 35.
[11] *Ibid.*, p. 37.

racial experience. If, then, we were to go back to any common man who lived six centuries ago or twelve centuries ago, we find that he lived in an age that was guided by basic beliefs and fixed standards, according to Bode; there was no democracy. Such was an aristocratic age and no common man and no race had experienced democracy. If people lived in conditions that would not be tolerated in a modern democracy, if the common man suffered fire, slaughter or degradation from his fellow man, to what right could he appeal for better treatment? Certainly not to the inalienable rights of human nature; there are none, according to Bode. Certainly not to individual or racial experience of justice and fair play as a guide for human conduct. At that time people took absolute standards as their guide or else followed their greed for power, riches, or pleasure. And thus Bode's philosophy would have left the common man without hope of betterment. It is only today when races have experienced democracy that the common man can appeal to the principles of this way of life in order to claim his rights and demand justice and fair play.

Have we any guarantee that man will always have the inalienable rights to life, liberty and the pursuit of happiness? Again Bode seems to answer in the negative.

> A democratic society governs itself by standards which are not absolute or fixed, but which are subject to change in the light of changing conditions and in accordance with the ideal of a

common life. . . . The characteristic trait of a genuine democracy is that it does not accept any given form of social organizations as necessarily final. . . . The point is, however, that the idea of democracy makes questions of right and wrong depend upon the consequences which our institutions and our actions have for associated human living.[12]

If we submit that future generations of common men will always have the right to life, liberty and the pursuit of happiness, we make a statement that is true now, will be true in the future and (if we further concede this right to common men of past ages— though it makes no difference to them now) was true in the past; in other words, here we have an absolute truth. This is at complete variance with Bode's thought where no absolutes are permitted. However, if we may not accept as absolutely true the statement we have made, we must draw the only conclusion that Bode leaves open for us, i.e., there may come a time when it will be false. There may come a time when democracy will not mean that each individual has the rights which the Constitution mentions. There may come a time when the statements contained in the Constitution will not be true. If someone argues that the Constitution does not contain truths but merely regulations, then we say that its aim is purely political, to set up a given form of social organization. Bode's thought would then seem to consider the Constitution doomed since democracy does not regard any social

[12] Bode, *Modern Educational Theories*, p. 68.

form as final. Basically, then, this champion for democracy seems to have evolved a philosophy to undermine American democracy as we know it.

So frequently does Bode reiterate his stand against absolutes that further criticism of his ideas is called for. He tells us that there is no middle way between traditionalism as the slave of absolutes and democracy, which is to be identified with relativism.[13] According to him, loyalty to the standards of absolute truth is irreconcilable with the democratic way of life.[14] The whole reason for his opposition seems to lie in the fact that the world we live in is in a state of flux, and social organization essentially demands flexibility.[15] In his arguments for the rejection of absolutes, our author makes use, perhaps unconsciously, of a type of faulty reasoning which was common among Darwinians in their defense of man's descent from apes.

> . . . if there is no absolute standard of judgment then our judgments must be made in terms of participation in common interests, regardless of other considerations. Conduct on the part of communities or of individuals must be evaluated with reference to its effect on promoting common interests among men. Liberty grows as the area of common interests is widened. Democracy becomes identified with this principle of relativity, as contrasted with the absolutism of dictatorships.[16]

[13] Bode, *Democracy as a Way of Life*, p. 48.
[14] Bode, *Progressive Education*, p. 29.
[15] Bode, *Democracy as a Way of Life*, p. 57.
[16] *Ibid.*, pp. 47–48.

Note that the quotation begins with an "if" clause, a supposition; as the author proceeds, he lets that supposition slide into the background and at the end of the passage he leaves the impression that he has proved something. Actually he has proved nothing; he has not tried to prove anything. He has made a statement, the truth of which depends on the non-existence of absolute standards. His statement could stand if he had already proved this non-existence. Examination of the preceding material gives no evidence of such proof.

In the preceding paragraphs, Bode gives instances of what he calls "an unquestioning, and sometimes even heroic, submission to a sacrosanct scheme of things when a wider sensitiveness to human values would seem to be more in accordance with good sense." [17] These instances are, briefly, Charles I's refusal to give way on the divine right of kings, the case of the Light Brigade rushing fearlessly and obediently into the valley of death, the social convention of not marrying outside one's class, the payment of gambling debts before all others, family feuds, the heeding of religion rather than science. The last example we do not consider for the moment as we shall have occasion to return to it. What of the others? Let us not forget that Bode is here working on an argument to show that traditional absolute standards of truth and morality are to be rejected. Surely a man of his keenness does not mean to suggest that these are some of the absolutes on which, for example, the

[17] *Ibid.*, pp. 46–47.

Catholic Church would build its way of life through the medium of the schools; that the whole tribe of absolutes are like these. The author displays faulty analysis and an ignorance of the doctrine of absolutes against which we think he is writing. If his rejection, however, means no more than the refusal to build society on such regulations as we call, not moral duties, but mere conventions, we confess that we are entirely with him. Conventions—man-made patterns of conduct as in the instances he cites—should be retained only when they do not clash with moral obligations, as long as they lead to a happier community life. We rejoice with Bode when some of these conventions are swept away in the flux of our modern world. But our agreement with Bode must stop here, because the bulk of his writing reveals that he means much more by absolutes than his present examples indicate.

Our author identifies democracy with the principle of relativism as contrasted with the absolutism of dictatorships.[18] There is here a hidden conclusion which the reader may draw without being aware of what he is doing. The conclusion is that loyalty to absolute truths means loyalty to the absolutism of dictatorships. This is a false assumption. The concept of absolutism has to do with the manner in which a belief is held; truth has to do with the content of that belief. A few examples may clarify the point. Dictatorship means that the state is above the individual, who must always give way to the good of the state.

[18] *Ibid.*, p. 48.

The Catholic Church holds that the state has authority over individuals but can never completely take away from individuals such inalienable rights as life, liberty and the pursuit of happiness. In both cases there is a question of absolutes. The first leads to concentration camps, the second to limitation of the state's power over individuals. The dictatorship of communism, for example, maintains that class warfare must continue until the successful establishment of the classless state. The Church holds that class warfare is always wrong, that capital needs labor and labor needs capital and therefore there should be mutual understanding between them. Here again we have absolutes; yet what a difference for the common man in whom Bode professes such interest. Seemingly our author has not analyzed very deeply the concepts against which he inveighs so bitterly. Although the Catholic Church teaches that some principles of life and conduct are absolutely true, she does not thereby automatically hold for the absolutism adopted by this or that political regime. If Bode is successful (and we hope he will be) in overthrowing the social appeal or imposition of dictatorships, the fundamental moral principles and beliefs of the Catholic Church will not therefore be cast into the historical waste-paper basket that has received so many false philosophies and ways of life in the past.

An extraordinary question appears in one of Bode's books. It calls for special comment.

What are these fundamental principles which

are so often mentioned and never explained or illustrated? [19]

The question is posed as part of a criticism of Dr. Hutchins' plea for educational reform. We do not intend to take up the cudgel on behalf of Mr. Hutchins; no doubt, he is well able to look after himself. In fact, we disagree with Hutchins on various points as we agree with Bode on others. However, we feel particularly involved here. Bode is criticizing the proposal to "cultivate devotion to eternal and immutable truth." [20] Paradoxically enough, Catholic educators are involved in this section of the argument by not being involved in Bode's consideration. Hutchins believes in eternal truth; so does the Catholic Church. The educational beliefs and principles of the former chancellor of the University of Chicago intimately affected one institution, because of his very position, and influenced a number of educators who have followed his lead; Catholic educational beliefs involve numerous universities and colleges, not only in the United States but throughout the world. Hutchins came to the front line within the last quarter of a century to battle for fundamental principles; the Church has upheld basic principles for twenty centuries. What must we think of the methodology of a writer who, in his desire to oust the way of life built on these fundamental principles, disposes of the matter in the following way? He attacks the writings

[19] Bode, *Progressive Education*, p. 31.
[20] *Ibid.*, p. 30.

40

and proposals of Hutchins and points out their weaknesses as he sees them. Then with Hutchins thus dethroned, he believes he has convinced all would-be followers of Aristotle and Thomas Aquinas that they are but "chasing rabbits." [21] Why should he waste time in considering any writings that may have emanated from these other sources? This is precisely the way Bode has acted on a very important philosophical question; it is a method that does not bear the stamp of a scholarly and scientific mind.

Let us, however, repeat Bode's question. Have these fundamental principles of frequent mention never been explained, never been illustrated? Whether Hutchins has done so or not is outside our consideration. Have Catholic educators been trying to build an educational system of their own without ever explaining or illustrating the reasons why they feel obliged to do so? What are the fundamental principles of this Catholic philosophy of education? What is meant by the claims for the good, the true and the beautiful? Perhaps a few examples of the eternal verities and basic beliefs might convince Bode that these concepts have not been kept in some great dark secrecy for all these years. Catholics consider it as eternally true that God exists, that God created man, that man is composed of body and soul, that man does not cease to be when his body has rotted in the grave, that man has free will and thus is responsible for many of his actions, that man can arrive at reliable knowledge and

[21] *Ibid.*, p. 30.

truth. Some of the fundamental moral principles can be mentioned too; since they are guides for action, they will greatly affect education. There are, for example, the Ten Commandments. Have they never been explained? It is too obvious that they have. Have they ever been illustrated? Catholic educators, for example, have pointed out time and again that children should not be exposed to an atmosphere filled with sex attractions, that sex instruction is not a matter for public and mixed classes of students. Another principle that flows from one of the commandments is that parents have prior right to the education of their children, a right that is not, however, derogatory to the social aspect of education in a particular nation or state.

It would be beyond the scope of this book to explain and defend the philosophy of Catholic education. That has been done and will be done again. It is nevertheless disconcerting to find a man of Bode's mental ability arguing repeatedly against Catholic principles while at the same time claiming that they were never explained nor illustrated. Bode gives no evidence that he looked for explanations and failed to find them. Let him disagree with us and say that our principles are hopelessly traditional and our so-called truths are false, which he actually does say; let him condemn our methods and say that they ill befit this age of science and democracy, which he also says repeatedly; let him reject our way of life, as he does in no uncertain way. But how can he honestly say that we have never explained nor illustrated our principles or beliefs, when Catholic books of philosophy, theology, education and sociology are full of explanations? We are sufficiently realistic not to expect Dr. Bode to agree that they are all good explanations; in fact, we would not be surprised to hear him say that none of them are good explanations. But they are explanations and we are in the position where we believe that they are good explanations. We also agree with Bode when he says that "the progressive movement has no monopoly of thinking." [22]

Some thoughtful reader may object to our emphasis of the Catholic position here. After all, Bode's question was, we recall, originally posed apropos of Hutchins' educational scheme and its underlying philosophy. The objection would be perfectly justified—under one condition. The condition is that somewhere in Bode's work we find a like consideration of the Catholic thought on fundamental absolutes. We go so far as to say that our author is intellectually obliged to offer that consideration, if scientific objectivity and free intelligence (so often mentioned by him) really mean anything to him. So positive a statement might be made in a more hesitant manner, if Bode never alluded to the Catholic Church, if it was a subject very far from his mind. This is not so; we find that the Catholic Church comes into his mind and into his writing quite frequently. Here is an illustration.

[22] *Ibid.*, p. 77.

> Perhaps it is not irrelevant to mention that a
> number of the early Romanticists, after a period
> of dissipation in the exercise of "freedom,"
> found an escape from the weight of chance de-
> sires by joining the Catholic Church.[23]

The unfortunate fate of these Romanticists as re-
ported by Bode will impress readers differently. A
Catholic might interpret the quotation thus. Such men
were to be pitied because the vagaries and excesses of
chance desires had brought them to a sorry pass. In a
blind rush to escape, they found an open door to the
Catholic Church. Here, however, was a haven which
could burden them only with absolute truths and
fixed standards—a fate not much better, perhaps even
worse, than that from which they had escaped. The
Catholic will be glad to state, of course, that his
Church does not close its doors to anyone. On the
other hand, he would know well that no adult is received as a convert merely by knocking on the door,
much less by rushing through that door with no clear
idea of where it leads. Anyone who has reached the
use of reason will be accepted as a convert only when
he shows that he knows what are the beliefs of the
Catholic Church, when he has grasped the reasonable
grounds on which those beliefs are based, and when
he is prepared to live up to the moral code of the
Catholic way of life. The guides to individual and
social action he gets to know through an explanation
of the Ten Commandments.

[23] *Ibid.*, pp. 99–100.

This process, according to Bode, apparently gives no chance for the exercise of free intelligence. An adult who "is hemmed in on all sides by bigotry and dogma . . ." [24] cannot be free intellectually. It is notorious that the Catholic Church teaches dogma; even Catholics admit that. Therefore it is to be presumed that the Catholic Church lives in an atmosphere of its own bigotry, a bigotry imbibed by any unfortunate convert who should enter its portals. But we can, with justice, retort that Bode teaches dogma. Is that possible? Dogma is a word that means doctrine. Bode's sphere is mainly educational and sociological while the sphere of the Catholic Church is primarily theological and moral. Yet Bode teaches that there is no life after death, that there is no room in a democracy for supreme attention to preparation for immortality;[25] he believes that there is no such thing as natural law which obliges men to carry out certain positive duties (for example, to obey lawful authority) and to avoid certain other actions (for example, murder); [26] Bode also holds that children should not be taught traditional basic beliefs.[27] The Catholic Church teaches that there is life after death, that in a true democracy the equality of men is a spiritual thing (it obviously is not material) because of their immortal souls. Catholic education fights for a system where children will be taught according to the fundamental

[24] *Ibid.*, p. 97.
[25] Bode, *Democracy as a Way of Life*, p. 70.
[26] Bode, *Progressive Education*, p. 35.
[27] *Ibid.*, p. 5.

principles that flow from man's nature. The similarity of matter contained in these contrary propositions of Bode and the Catholic Church is evident. If one is dogma, the other is dogma.

The whole trouble with the word "dogma" is that it carries an emotional overtone. In past times, there have been persecutions because of religious beliefs; ministers of religion have done deeds of cruelty in supposed defense of their beliefs. These beliefs are dogma; therefore, cruelty is a necessary consequence of dogma. This argument can, of course, cut another way. The great ideals of democracy—liberty, equality, fraternity—were first forcefully championed in 1789 by men who proceeded to send all their enemies and many of their friends to the guillotine. Is terrorism then a necessary consequence of the principles of democracy? The answer is obvious, but the question is still pertinent because men are still killing others today to uphold democratic principles.

As a matter of fact, Bode's aim, on behalf of progressive education and democracy, is to give them a dogma, a set of underlying beliefs on which can be built a way of life. Surely nothing could make our author happier than to convince people to adopt his democratic principles and standards in such a wholehearted way that they would be prepared to sacrifice themselves, if need be, for democracy. It is true that he repeats time and again that his standards are not fixed and absolute. It is true that he maintains that the true democratic teacher should not aim at making converts.

> The teacher's work is done when he has made the issue clear as best he can. Education becomes propaganda when we set out deliberately to make converts.[28]

This seems to offer an unusual anomaly. Bode believes in democracy with all his heart; he considers that progressive education, constructed on an underlying philosophy, will make democracy secure for the future. Yet he does not want to make converts to his cause; that would be propaganda. He would like converts to his cause but he would not like to make converts to his cause. It is all very confusing.

In a democratic social order, there must be a distinctive system of education; hence, the school is probably the most important single factor for Bode in the reconstruction he aims at. In his schools there will be no indoctrination. This method of teaching, often adopted by religious bodies, according to Bode, has no place in a social order which is to free intelligence for right thinking. Our author seems to offer contradictory ideas on right and wrong thinking.

> The emphasis of progressive education on the individual, on the sinfulness of "imposition," and on the necessity of securing free play for intelligence, *whether rightly or wrongly applied*, is

[28] *Ibid.*, p. 81.

a reflection of the growing demand, outside of
school, for recognition of the common man.[29]
[Italics added.]

The application of intelligence implies thinking; yet
this passage seems to recommend nothing more than
the application of intelligence, regardless of whether
the resultant thinking be right or wrong. Another
statement of the author seems to insist on right thinking only.

> But it is necessary to go further and protect
> growth against wrong thinking.[30]

We may find ourselves confused by such language;
we may also notice confusion in Bode's standards for
judging between good and bad desires, real and ficti-
tious needs, between desirable and undesirable social
relations. We cannot, however, have any confusion
about Bode's thought on imposition or indoctrination.
It seems evident to him that those who indulge in
theology can never have real freedom of intellect. But
he wishes it to be clearly understood that coming to
grips with the real issue between democracy and
tradition, namely, denial of all absolutes, is no more
indoctrination than is the discussion of any other
topic.[31] It is especially interesting for those who are
supposedly caught in the snares of theological superstition to compare Bode's declaration of democracy

[29] *Ibid.*, p. 11.
[30] *Ibid.*, p. 77.
[31] *Ibid.*, p. 81.

with the oft-accused dogmatism of the Catholic Church.

> A democratic program of education must necessarily rest on the perception that democracy is a challenge to all forms of absolutism, that it has its own standards, ideals, and values, and that these must pervade the entire program from end to end.[32]

The temptation to italicize all the words denoting dogmatic obligation was almost too great to be resisted. Yet, even without italics to catch his eye, a discerning reader will note that the whole passage is cast in a tone that denotes imposition. The argument seems to be something like this. Do this or democracy fails. No one who values democracy wants it to fail. Therefore. Let us now examine how the Church's dogmatism works. Do this or lose your soul. No one who is convinced that he has an immortal soul wishes to lose it. Therefore. The ordinary reader would detect a great similarity of dogmatism. Bode himself is not very fortunate in trying to show that there is a difference.

> In brief, there is a world of difference between conformity to a standard because there is in the background the menace of a club and conformity because the thing to which we conform belongs to a frame of reference which we accept and use as a means for the organization of thought and conduct.[33]

[32] *Ibid.*, p. 39.
[33] Bode, *Democracy as a Way of Life*, p. 45.

There seems to be one unshakeable absolute in Bode's mind, unshakeable even by experimental evidence, so unshakeable, indeed, that Bode does not look for experimental evidence. That absolute claims that the only reason for belief in religion is the menace of a club that enforces belief. We are led to suspect further a strong myopic tendency in Bode's thought when we find the following declaration about his own democratic education.

> Whether or not this type of education is called indoctrination is not nearly so important as the recognition that it has a quality all its own.[34]

Theology, in Bode's estimation, bars the door to any development.[35] New knowledge and new methods are shut out by the bigotry of dogma.[36] These are arresting statements to people who not only believe in theology but who have forsaken other ways of living to devote themselves to the spread of Christianity. Catholic priests have done this. They do it without any menace of a club, except that club under whose blows so many of them are falling in communist countries. Priests are given a long and rigorous intellectual training. Our author is committed to the view that such training is not even intelligent, that the way of living that flows from it is neither free nor democratic. Perhaps we will be pardoned for pointing out

[34] *Ibid.*, p. 104.
[35] Bode, *Progressive Education*, p. 51.
[36] *Ibid.*, p. 97.

the general qualities of character required in priests, the professional knowledge necessary, as expressly treated in various papal encyclicals. Pius XI, for example, dwelt at some length on the sacred sciences with which the priest must be familiar. But the Holy Father demands more:

> Yet even more is required. The dignity of the office he holds, the maintenance of a becoming respect and esteem among the people, which helps so much in his pastoral work, demand more than purely ecclesiastical learning. The priest must be graced by no less knowledge and culture than is usual among well-bred and well-educated people of his day. This is to say that he must be healthily modern, as is the Church which is at home in all times and in all places, and adapts itself to all: which blesses and furthers all healthy initiative and has no fear of the progress, even the most daring progress of science, if only it be true science.[37]

There are in the United States many Catholic theological seminaries for the training of priests. They are the evidence which may be examined and should be examined before any indictment is made of "adults hemmed in by bigotry and dogma." Bode indeed believes that our civilization is too much impregnated with absolutist beliefs to give hope that they will be easily laid aside. Thereby he reveals his expectation

[37] Pius XI, *The Catholic Priesthood: An Encyclical Letter* (Washington, D. C.: National Catholic Welfare Conference, 1936), pp. 40–41.

of opposition to his own views and program. Catholic theology, the Catholic moral code, Catholic values have often been attacked. Yet an investigation of firsthand complete evidence will dispel all difficulties for the sincere student. We expect sincere investigation, especially from men of high intellectual stature.

The evidence we have adduced in this chapter seems to show that Bode is not true to his own principles of free intelligent thinking and criticism; neither is he consistent in his own thought. In conclusion, let us examine one more argument he uses in partial defense, at least, of the value of progressive education.

> Nevertheless, the revolt against traditionalism in education is too widespread and too persistent to be dismissed as due to the vagaries of modern pedagogy.[38]

This argument seems to be more telling against his own cause than against his philosophical opponents. Catholicism is a way of life that is much more widespread and persistent than progressivism has shown itself to be; belief in theological and traditional moral values is even more widespread than Catholicism; belief in democracy as founded on the intrinsic nature of man rather than on the developing experience or "operational concepts" of the race is more widespread than is Bode's idea of democracy. How then can these be dismissed as the vagaries of Church and creed,

[38] Bode, *Progressive Education*, p. 90.

the battle-cries of brief dictatorships, or the fanaticism of bigoted priests?

The cardinal error of Bode's philosophy lies in his concept of change. He realizes that we live in a world of flux, that changing conditions demand a change in our way of life. He does not seem to understand that change and permanence together go to build up a sound social order. Even on this point we find some contradiction in his thought for he wishes the school to hand on what is really valuable in racial experience.[39] The corollary of Bode's cardinal error is his contention that a belief in absolutes denies all possibility of change or adaptation to new conditions. By such faulty analysis, our author's philosophy follows a path to topsy-turvydom, though he had hoped to give guidance to a world that was never more lacking in a sense of direction,[40] "such guidance or leadership as its professional educators can give." [41]

[39] Bode, *Educational Theories*, p. 34.
[40] Bode, *Democracy as a Way of Life*, p. 32.
[41] Bode, *Educational Theories*, p. 113.

Chapter Three... CHILDS AND OTHERS: PHILOSOPHERS OF EXPERIMENTALISM

As the years passed and the progressive movement took deeper root, the earlier leaders yielded place to younger men. It is not surprising that a man like John L. Childs soon became a top leader in this school of philosophy. His output of writing, since he joined the faculty at Teachers College, Columbia University, is evidence enough that he holds an undoubted prominence among the progressives. He has given us two expositions of the philosophy of experimentalism. These we shall study to find out how faithful this author has been to the principles that he professes.

1

It is possible that Childs would be surprised to find that he is at one with Catholic ideas in a great deal of his thinking; even in some of the philosophic background of his experimentalism there would be no disagreement with Catholic teaching. Catholics will readily admit that the progressives were the leaders in this century in advocating many valuable educational techniques that have superseded earlier teaching methods. Not only that, but it is clear that the leading thinkers of the pragmatist school have fundamentally agreed with Catholics in their criticism of progressive educational excesses that presented experimental practice as chaos rather than education. These excesses they condemned; the dangers they continually pointed out in the hope of avoiding further ridiculous interpretations of their doctrine. We can easily indicate some of the points on which we agree with Childs.

We agree, for instance, that conscience is not an infallible guide in moral matters nor is the sphere of morality separated from ordinary life.[1] We also agree that intelligence is not "a supernatural intrusion into the natural scene."[2] Education, for the Catholic as for the experimentalist, is not just a means of pouring useful information into the individual.[3] We recognize, too, that education can be so concerned in indoctrinating children with accepted moral and religious beliefs as to fail to develop initiative and independent thinking.[4] Education can also be used to implant immoral, irreligious, political, economic and educational beliefs. Education in our thought is life-long [5] and we agree that the schools have been set up to aid this process during a very influential period of life.[6] There can be no doubt that modern psychology has failed to find any training which will justify the substitution of rote behavior in place of intelligent understanding of activity; disaster will certainly ensue if rote behavior

[1] John L. Childs, *Education and the Philosophy of Experimentalism* (New York: Appleton-Century-Crofts, Inc., 1931), p. 109.

[2] *Ibid.*, p. 76.

[3] *Ibid.*, p. 135.

[4] *Ibid.*, p. 141.

[5] *Ibid.*, p. 128.

[6] *Ibid.*, p. 129.

is the only procedure for human activity in our changing world.[7]

Neither Childs nor any Catholic educator will take these points of agreement as indications that experimental and Catholic philosophy are really in fundamental agreement. For experimental thought to be a philosophy, Childs recognizes that it must have something to say about the nature of man and of the world in which he lives. What experimentalism says on these subjects lays the foundations for disagreement. It is not our present purpose to criticize the principles of experimentalism but rather to complain of Child's unscholarly dismissal of our Catholic philosophy of education. He does not accord us the academic courtesy he demands for his own theories. He says:

> Whatever may be our final judgment as to the worth of the philosophy . . . its position in the modern world is such as to warrant that its critics take pains to try to understand it before they dismiss it. . . .[8] Harm is done, however, when a description or analysis made from one point of view is assumed to be the only possible construction which can be put upon the findings, and hasty educational programs are set up on the basis of these partial interpretations.[9]

In the first quotation, the author is speaking of the philosophy of experimentalism and in the second he

[7] *Ibid.*, p. 216.
[8] *Ibid.*, p. 18.
[9] *Ibid.*, p. 215.

is referring to certain researches of some modern psychologists. Catholic educators can justly demand the same treatment from the progressives which Childs demands from the psychologists whom he criticizes. Catholic educational writers would have Dewey's followers try to understand Catholic philosophy before dismissing it. It would seem the duty of a scientific and objective inquirer (and this is a duty laid down, not by the moral law only, but by the laws of experimental methodology) to note these points of agreement between diverging philosophies. Childs himself does not fail to bring to notice the points of disagreement. In his present work, the duty we mention has not been fulfilled. The disagreement is noted and emphasized; the agreement is ignored.

Our author does not mention by name either Catholic tradition or Catholic education. Yet he makes veiled references and insinuations and it is well to examine these passages since such oblique and unscientific criticism and accusation is characteristic of modern educational writing in reference to Catholic education and philosophy. Catholics, of course, are not the only target of such sniping. Examples of indirect attacks on Catholic thought are, however, numerous. Childs confidently asserts that supernaturalisms of all sorts are untenable;[10] this, apparently, should be quite obvious from the teaching of experimental philosophy without bringing forward any sort of proof. Sectarian schools of the United

[10] *Ibid.*, p. 46.

States, says the author, are on a par with the schools of totalitarian countries in using education for ulterior purposes.[11] Childs has no doubt whatever when he makes this statement nor does he mean to withdraw this indictment in the following declaration made on the same page, as is clear from the context.

> Possibly he [the experimentalist] has been too prone to assume that those who oppose certain methods of educating for freedom must be inspired by a desire to manipulate the lives of children for selfish private purposes of their own. That frequently such motives operate cannot be doubted, but this is not always the case.[12]

This totalitarian accusation touches many Americans; there should be evidence to back up the charge. Childs should be able to show from a fair sampling of the many millions who have passed through Catholic schools (and those of other religious bodies) that they had no experience of freedom, that they were not trained to think independently, that they never got the chance of knowing anything beyond the narrow limits that are supposedly set up by belief in any absolute truths. In presenting such evidence (of which there is no trace in his work), our author should not be led to suppress the testimony of those who might look back with profound gratitude to their Catholic education. He is also welcome to produce what evi-

[11] *Ibid.*, p. 143.
[12] *Ibid.*

dence he may find from Catholics who condemn Catholic education. With experimental procedure of this kind, there would be opportunity to test his findings. Childs has acted far otherwise; he asserts and accuses without evidence and leaves the accusation to work what harm it may.

Traditional dualism has been the source of a pernicious influence in education, according to the thought of our author.[13] Such dualism means the belief that man is composed of body and soul; progressives, on the other hand, teach that man is continuous with nature. "Pernicious" is a strong word to use, especially when we find that the belief which is to replace dualism is inconsistent, as in Childs' writings. To say that man is continuous with nature means that individuality is born of the interaction between an animal organism, albeit a complex one, and environment.[14] It is true that the author makes claim, in the following quotation, for more than a biological organism.

> Now the experimentalist does see man as a biological organism but he also sees man as a human being capable of all that which makes a refined humane experience possible.[15]

There is no antithesis in these two claims, according to Childs. Man is different from an animal that cannot conceive ideas. Intelligence is merely behavior guided by anticipated consequences.[16]

[13] *Ibid.*, p. 76.
[14] *Ibid.*, p. 84; cf. also p. 87.
[15] *Ibid.*, p. 70.
[16] *Ibid.*, p. 75.

> When is behavior intellectual? The simple
> answer of the experimentalist is, when "it knows
> what it is about"—when it knows what can be
> expected of things and what can be done with
> them.[17]

Anticipated consequences must be anticipated by a subject; this subject cannot be behavior which is not yet actualized. How can any activity "know what it is about"? The answer of the experimentalist may seem simple to Childs. What he does not realize is that in his attempt to explain away the dualism of body and soul, he is caught up in the very phraseology and concepts which owe their validity to the original concept of mind and body. No *sub-human animal* is capable of rising to man's thinking activities which, as our author himself says, are something more than physical experiences. A biological organism is capable only of physical experiences; mere complexity on a biological level still does not raise an organism above physical experience. Childs sees a difference between the experiences of men and animals but has not the courage to admit that it is an essential difference, one that demands in man a subject capable of activity that is more than physical. Such a difference does not cause us to conceive man as something like a monkey in a cage, with a sort of unnatural oneness. With regard to human activity either of a spiritual or of a bodily kind, the concept of dualism does not postulate two subjects, one the spiritual soul separated from

[17] *Ibid.*, p. 74.

reality, the other the biological organism in contact with reality. In traditional philosophy as taught in Catholic schools, there is the one active subject, the human person.

In experimental philosophy as expounded by Childs, it seems that there cannot be such a thing as human personality. In view of the fact that he speaks of the profound respect of experimentalism for human individuality,[18] this may sound an extraordinary statement. Our author does not admit the Thomist distinction whereby any single, undivided, incommunicably existing, and complete entity is called an individual but a person is any single, undivided, incommunicably existing, and complete entity *of a rational nature*, an intellectual individual with at least the radical power to think. In Childs' philosophy, such a distinction is not possible. Readers, however, might carry away the impression that, when he speaks of individuality, he means the human person of which even our senses make us aware. Yet that cannot be in his philosophy any more than can be the Thomist distinction.

> Individuality is not an original datum, it is an achievement. . . .[19] Through the process of experiencing, the child literally becomes a self. . . .[20] In its broad sense, the experimentalist conceives education to be that total process by

[18] *Ibid.*, p. 227.
[19] *Ibid.*, p. 85.
[20] *Ibid.* Cf. also *loc. cit.*: "Through shared experience he becomes a person."

which we become individuals. . . .[21] the experimentalist sees man becoming a human being through his interaction with an environment. . . .[22] Individuals are individuals by virtue of the fact that they are born into a social environment and achieve individuality through its nurturing influence.[23]

We are sufficiently familiar with Childs' ideas on education to know that, for him, it is a process that does not stop at any period of an individual's life; it is "ongoing experience" in the sense that it goes on though it may not be sure where. One question we would like to ask. At what particular stage of this process do these "animals of a certain complex structure grow into human beings"? [24] "Children are not to be viewed as mere immature adults," [25] according to our author. We agree with this statement in the hope that Childs meant what he said. An immature adult is an adult whose rational development did not keep pace with his physical growth in the normal passing of years. No child can be viewed as such. But we do think that the child is a human person whose powers are developing through experience and, with this continuing development, the child will become a mature adult. In our view, the child has personality; it is not clear that such a "complex animal" ever has

21 *Ibid.*, p. 135.
22 *Ibid.*, p. 84.
23 *Ibid.*, p. 88.
24 *Ibid.*, p. 87.
25 *Ibid.*, p. 231.

personality in Childs' philosophy. According to his teaching, individuality is an achievement. Achievement is something final. Yet at one time we are told that there can be nothing final; [26] at another time we learn that finalities are possible.[27]

Further inconsistency in our author's concept of individuality in human beings is revealed by analysis of another of his statements.

> Its understanding of the psychology of the self leads experimentalism to reject any theory of education founded on the principle that education is a process of natural unfolding of inborn capacities. The self develops out of its experiences.[28]

We think we interpret his thought correctly by saying that Childs hardly considered that anyone would build a theory of education on the concept of natural capacities unfolding without any influence except what comes from the individual in question. Such a view would be ridiculous. On the contrary, Childs seems to be opposing strongly the concept of inborn capacities. His substitute is the development of the self out of its experiences. Here again we meet a real difficulty in knowing what the writer means by "development." An acorn, in suitable conditions which we know, will develop into an oak. There is in the acorn an inborn capacity to become a particular kind

[26] *Ibid.*, p. 256.
[27] *Ibid.*, p. 252.
[28] *Ibid.*, p. 160.

of tree, given the right environment and experiences. Does the "complex animal," which seems to be Childs' original datum, become a person in a somewhat similar way by the development of natural capacities? Childs denies such a development since he denies inborn capacities. We are led to think, then, that Childs has a different meaning for "develop." His thought seems to be that the self becomes a self by its experiences. If this be the true interpretation of his thought, then that thought is most inconsistent. The self is a self if it has experiences—it does not become a self by experience. If the author can produce evidence to show how any living animal can become something else through experience and not because of the development of inborn or natural capacities, his statement might be worth some consideration. He has produced no such evidence. Nor does he think it worth while to mention that Catholic philosophy in no way minimizes the tremendous effect of environment or social milieu on the development of personality. What Catholic philosophy emphasizes most of all is that there is a personality to develop.

It is taken for granted by Childs that all traditional ideas, especially moral and religious beliefs, are handed down and received without possibility of the learner appreciating their reasonableness. In the mind of this author, there seems to be no alternative to rote learning and rote behavior in a traditional system of education or a religious way of life.[29] On the other hand, he

[29] *Ibid.*, p. 128.

believes that science and its method cannot be gainsaid; they have earned their authority.[30] He does not consider any evidence that moral and religious principles have earned their authority. Such evidence can be found by a mere historical and sociological investigation into the lives of nations; it is not necessary, for this purpose, to appeal to the authority of God and His revelation—the final basis of religion. The consequences [31] of living up to traditional morality and its principles are facts of history that can be verified. Childs does not consider these facts. He does consider the failure of people and nations to live up to these standards as sufficient reason for rejecting the standards—another example of his logical sleight-of-hand in presenting argumentation. Our author agrees with Walter Lippmann, who contends that relying on fixed codes is foolish "because so to do is to attempt the impossible." [32] The only answer we give to this statement is that the attempt has been made and has been successful.

Childs' idea of fixed standards seems to be that they are appraised "in terms of their ancient origin." [33] That fixed standards are foolish seems, in his mind, to be clearly demonstrated by the fact that "even such a simple activity as crossing the street cannot be safely reduced to a fixed routine." [34] What a complete over-

[30] *Ibid.*, p. 112.
[31] *Ibid.*, p. 115. Childs places great value on consequences.
[32] *Ibid.*, p. 183.
[33] *Ibid.*, p. 183.
[34] *Ibid.*, p. 186.

throw of the absolute principles to which Catholic philosophy and religion cling so desperately! In fact, it is impossible to understand how the millions of American Catholics alive today can be alive; they have been taught in those "sectarian schools" which Childs dislikes; they have had fixed ideas and hence must have been "controlled by static rather than dynamic notions";[35] they have, according to our author, been educated only to rote behavior; yet they have been crossing the streets of every busy American city every day of their lives without any greater proportion of fatalities than any other section of the population. As a matter of fact, a small and simple application of the scientific method would have saved Childs from these implications involved in his attack on fixed ends and rote behavior. He could have gone out and asked any Catholic police-officer or taxi-driver in New York City whether such police-officer or cab-driver was constrained, because of his Catholic education, to reduce to a fixed routine the process of crossing the street. We could, of course, give a more philosophic answer to Childs' example of street-crossing; it can easily be shown that general principles can be given as guidance for conduct involved in this activity. However, such a philosophic answer would not be acceptable to our author, as will be obvious from the following quotation:

> We do not behave in general, we do not face problems in general. Conduct is always an affair

[35] *Ibid.*, p. 244.

of particulars. If this be true, we cannot give guidance in general.[36]

It must in fairness be admitted that other words of the author seem to take away the force of this statement. If we were to judge by these other passages, Childs does not really wish to cast out general principles as guides to conduct; he clearly says so:

> On the other hand, it cannot be doubted that experimentalism does have general guiding principles with respect to the function of adults in educational procedures relating to children.[37]

But if Childs makes this admission (as he actually does), he is right back with a system of morality, secular though it be. When adults function, they are active, they are engaged in experience; their actions can be called conduct or behavior, and that behavior, according to the quotation, is guided by general principles. Not only are general principles thus re-introduced; this quotation brings back another concept not much loved by progressives—the concept of authority.[38] If adults must act according to these basic principles, authority is being laid on them from some outside source; if, as Childs says, the adult teacher is not relieved from "a certain responsibility for final outcomes," [39] then authority is being imposed in some way upon the children.

[36] *Ibid.*, p. 130.
[37] *Ibid.*, p. 159.
[38] *Ibid.*, p. 90.
[39] *Ibid.*, p. 130.

It is hardly necessary to produce further examples of inconsistency and unscientific and unobjective procedures from this first exposition of our author's philosophy. Such deficiencies are, however, revealed in his concepts of ideals,[40] stability and change,[41] freedom and free will [42] (though we salute him for even introducing this last topic); nor does it seem worth while to draw attention to the omissions in his delineations of traditional philosophies,[43] in his consideration of ordinary life experiences as a test for conduct [44] with no mention of extraordinary experiences which in our era enter greatly into millions of lives. With him we say "the true is the verified." [45] He has verified very little in the hidden implications or open accusations against traditional morality and religion. We can agree with the judgment he passes on his own work:

> As we come to the conclusion of this discussion of experimentalism, the conviction deepens that there is no conclusion in any important sense . . .[46] so also must it be admitted that no insight or statement by any of the prophetic leaders of experimentalism can ever be taken as final.[47]

[40] *Ibid.*, pp. 59, 177.
[41] *Ibid.*, *passim.*
[42] *Ibid.*, pp. 144 ff.
[43] *Ibid.*, pp. 97–98.
[44] *Ibid.*, pp. 51, 97.
[45] *Ibid.*, p. 79.
[46] *Ibid.*, p. 255.
[47] *Ibid.*, p. 256.

2

After a lapse of twenty eventful years, John L. Childs set forth a second exposition of the philosophy of progressive educators. These years were eventful because they covered two very important eras in the development of American society. The first era was that of the depression and this lasted until the outbreak of World War II brought with it a period of artificial prosperity. During the years of this period, great changes were taking place in the economic life of the people. Labor was given the rights of a natural child in the social and economic life of the United States and thus left behind, at least for the time being, the days of existing as a badly persecuted and unwanted step-child. On September 3, 1939, the war that had been threatening in Europe for so long came finally to the point of eruption. Within a short few years, the United States was involved. From that time onwards, it became increasingly clear that it was no mere physical war between armies but a battle between basic philosophies of life. In this second era, the importance of democracy as a way of life was more and more emphasized; with the end of hostilities and the cessation of an uneasy fighting partnership with the worst dictatorship the world has known, American democracy found itself involved in a life and death struggle for survival. To all men of thought, like Childs, the school and education rightly assume great importance in this democratic struggle. Hence our author thought it fitting to propose his philosophy under the title *Education and Morals: An Experimental Philosophy of Education.* There is much of value in this book and we do not wish to minimize the importance of such material. Yet we are obliged to criticize it for the same shortcomings noted in the earlier book. Our main concern is to show that Childs, a scientific thinker who insists on the need for free inquiry, scientific method, and the presentation of alternatives, is not true to the principles he advocates.

In this new book, Childs mentions the Catholic Church specifically.

> . . . today in the field of education, the leaders of the Roman Catholic Church claim that the right of the Church to enroll all of its children in its own system of parochial schools is a "natural right," subject to no review or restriction by any agency whatsoever. . . .[48]

We admit that the Church claims the right to enroll all its children in Catholic schools. In fact, because she believes in the existence of this right, the Church will oppose the current interpretation of the First Amendment which holds for such a complete separation of Church and State that it is considered unconstitutional by some to permit specified American citizens to ride on a school bus provided for by public funds. We can see the point of view of men like Childs in their op-

[48] John L. Childs, *Education and Morals: An Experimental Philosophy of Education* (New York: Appleton-Century-Crofts, Inc., 1950), p. 97.

position to Catholic education. We can grant the reasonableness and justice of that opposition if the Catholic Church teaches what these men thinks she teaches. We can excuse the hatred that is so often invoked against the Catholic Church if she makes claims such as Childs has mentioned. However, our love for intellectual freedom, our zeal for objectivity and our devotion to scientific method lead us to believe that the best way of finding out what the Catholic Church teaches is to listen to her teaching, to read her teaching, to see her principles of belief and conduct applied in practice. That we can trust even intellectual men like our author to make correct interpretations from simple reading seems impossible. As evidence, we offer a quotation from Pius XI on the subject of the Church's rights in education.

> Over and above this, the State can exact, and take measures to secure that all its citizens have the necessary knowledge of their civic and political duties, and a degree of physical, intellectual and moral culture, which, considering the conditions of our times, is really necessary for the common good.[49]

A casual reader will easily see that, whatever rights the Church may claim in education, these rights are restricted in some way by what the Church teaches to be the rights of the state. One would expect, and

---

[49] Pius XI, "Encyclical Letter on the Christian Education of Youth," *Five Great Encyclicals* (New York: The Paulist Press, 1939), p. 49.

surely it is not asking too much, that a man of Childs' intellectual stature would have taken the trouble to read the thirty pages that comprise the pronouncement on the Catholic Church's official stand on education by the highest authority and first leader of that Church.

Childs grants to Catholics the constitutional right to desire and set up schools of their own. His concession accords with the decision of the Federal Supreme Court in the famous Oregon School Case in 1925. The judgment arose out of a law passed in Oregon which obliged all parents and those who had control of children to send them to the public school while it was in session in their district. This statute, an amendment to a previous law, made some exceptions but omitted from those exceptions children receiving equivalent education in private schools. These children had been excepted from observance of the earlier law. The omission in the new regulation caused a group of Catholic teaching Sisters (who had taught school in Oregon for forty years before) to obtain an injunction against the defendants of the case, namely, the Governor of Oregon and his Attorney-General, to prevent them from attempting to enforce the law. When the case came before the Supreme Court, judgment was given in favor of the Sisters.[50] This judgment forces men like Childs to recognize a right they would like to deny, the right of Catholic parents to

[50] *Oregon School Case: Complete Record* (Baltimore: The Belvedere Press, Inc., 1925), p. 941.

send their children to Catholic schools. That our author would like to deny this right seems fairly evident; he shows some hesitation in approving its exercise and says that the state must have the ultimate right to see that children develop "the attitudes and the allegiances that are necessary to the maintenance of our democratic society." [51] At the end of a fairly good section on the Catholic position with regard to parochial schools,[52] Childs notes that not all Catholics agree with the Church's official pronouncement on the matter.[53] That is true; it is not true, as seems to be implied, that such people constitute a noticeable body of the Catholic faithful.

Logic and consistency of thought should compel our author to support the Catholic position.

> We are convinced that the character of the program of education which the schools will provide during this time of transition will be determined ultimately by what American parents want for their children. . . .[54] In the main, the more that parents are responsible for the making of specific policies for the education of their own children, the more democratic our educational controls are likely to be. . . .[55]

Catholic parents do want parochial schools for their children. Our author, however, insinuates that their

[51] Childs, *op. cit.*, p. 253.
[52] *Ibid.*, pp. 245–250.
[53] *Ibid.*, p. 250.
[54] *Ibid.*, p. 126.
[55] *Ibid.*, p. 260.

freedom in making this choice is too greatly influenced by the clergy to make it a valid choice.[56] Since, according to Childs, this is so, their wishes as American parents must be discounted. Nevertheless Catholics can recognize, with just as much assurance as any progressive philosopher, that the major problem of education is to determine the "patterns of life and thought in which the young are to be nurtured." [57] They know also that the young must be directed and that adults must do the directing;[58] they realize that education means more than presenting alternatives, that educators must be responsible for helping pupils to see the crucial factors in life;[59] they see that "all education is inescapably a form of character education." [60] The pivotal point on which Catholics demand schools of their own is, to use Childs' words, "that the moral interest pervades the entire educational program." [61]

We note with interest what seems to be a development of the author's thought on one point during the twenty-year span between his publications. Recall that he objected to considering children "mere immature adults." We agreed with the obvious interpretation contained in his objection but found difficulty in knowing what precisely he meant by the develop-

[56] *Ibid.*, p. 250.
[57] *Ibid.*, p. 264.
[58] *Ibid.*, pp. 6, 15.
[59] *Ibid.*, p. 129.
[60] *Ibid.*, p. 167.
[61] *Ibid.*, p. 17; cf. also p. 266.

ment of personality or self. He has something further to say about it in this later work.

> Educators must respond not with glittering generalities, but with definite encouragements and discouragements, with concrete approvals and disapprovals, as the young, under their guidance, live and learn and progressively *mature* their habits of thought and behavior. . . .[62] Whoever seeks to have the young acquire beliefs without at the same time providing suitable opportunity for them to inquire into the grounds of those beliefs is negating the process by which the young *mature* into morally responsible—reflective—human beings.[63] [Italics added.]

Childs makes a profession of faith in fair-mindedness and in the value of objectivity; this we would like to quote.

> Beliefs from any source are welcome provided that their sponsors are prepared to have their credentials put to the test of operational procedure. . . .[64] The authority of the expert is an authority that rests, in the last analysis, on the empirical and public character of the methods by which he works and produces his results.[65]

It is not easy to determine what the author means by "operational procedure." If the phrase means the laws

[62] *Ibid.*, p. 49.
[63] *Ibid.*, p. 186.
[64] *Ibid.*, p. 174.
[65] *Ibid.*, p. 175.

of critical thought and inquiry, then Catholic beliefs must be very welcome. Has Childs himself shown sufficient credentials for his condemnation of the three million pupils in Catholic schools, and of the millions of Americans who have been educated in religious schools since the experimentalists first entered the educational field some fifty years ago? Has he shown that Catholic children are not as well trained in all the values he proposes as being particularly democratic? Has he shown that Catholic parents are an inferior brand of Americans? Has he shown that the graduates of Catholic schools and colleges display a patriotism that is not truly American? This is the belief he proposes.

> Obviously, to the extent that these groups withdraw their children from the common school, that school is prevented from giving American children the richest possible experience of community.[66]

The worth of a policy in a democratic society is best tested, according to Childs, by the fruits of that policy. He should therefore be prepared to find out by operational procedure, by public methods, whether the product of the Catholic grade or high school, of the Catholic college or university, is inferior to the product of the public school or of the state university.

Divine revelation and absolute standards of morality come in for their share of condemnation in this book,

[66] *Ibid.*, p. 242.

as in most progressive publications. They are considered to be nothing more than "an irrelevance or an intolerable interference." [67] The author wants, instead, a morality that is conscious of the changing nature of society, of the new situations that arise in modern social and economic life.

> We need a morality today that is actively concerned with the organization and the control of our industrialized ways of making a living, with the development of more just conditions for minority racial and religious groups, and with the modification of the role of the nation-state in an interdependent world equipped with scientific means of mass destruction. [68]

Childs has discovered that, because the world has become so interdependent, the owner can no longer do what he pleases with his property or wealth;[69] there are social obligations to ownership. In this instance, we find another example of the author's inability to pursue his own method of scientific inquiry. Traditional morality is condemned by him for not being alive to such a problem. Let us, however, quote from a thirteenth century exponent of that traditional morality, an exponent who should be recognized as sufficiently representative.

Man should not consider his outward possessions

[67] *Ibid.*, p. 44.
[68] *Ibid.*, p. 266.
[69] *Ibid.*, p. 30.

> as his own, but as common to all, so as to share
> them without difficulty when others are in
> need. Whence the Apostle said, Command the
> rich of this world . . . to give with ease, to
> communicate.[70]

The context of this quotation makes it quite clear that
St. Thomas does not attack the right to private property but lays social obligations on the use of that
property. If the thirteenth century is too distant for
Childs' inquiring mind, he can find a more modern
exponent of the same doctrine. Leo XIII, in his encyclical on the condition of the working classes,[71]
gives a clear exposition of the moral obligation which
our author thinks progressivism has discovered.
Furthermore, any text-book of Catholic moral theology will teach the same principle.

For experimentalists, ideas must lead to action; it is
perhaps not sufficient for them to see these moral
principles in writing. But the happy fact is that the
ideas of St. Thomas, Leo XIII, and Catholic theo-
logians in general, have not remained sterile. Sufficient
evidence can be found in the activity of the Church,
championing the worker in his unjust state of servitude. While the reign of sweatshops seems to have
disappeared in the United States, labor relations is
even yet a field of much contention. We would ask
Childs to take a look at what the various Catholic

---

[70] St. Thomas Aquinas, *Summa Theologica*, 2a 2ae, Q. lxvi, art.
2.

[71] *Five Great Encyclicals*, p. 11.

diocesan Labor Schools are doing to forge good relations between management and labor. Lest our testimony be considered biased, we refer to a public tribute [72] paid by two experts in this sphere to the work being done by those "undemocratic" (according to Childs) Americans who constitute the Catholic priesthood of the United States.

Like many experimentalists, Childs makes an unwarranted assumption that Catholic priests never emerge from the confines of what he would probably consider the musty tomes of a worn-out medieval theology. He takes it for granted that their acceptance of theological truths is not logically premised by an investigation of the reasonableness of the grounds for believing. The word "logical" is used advisedly because we do not mean to contend that those priests, as children, learned their Catechism with the amount of argumentation that is required in their professional study of theology. These clergy are as much children of this modern go-ahead world as is Childs. There was, it is true, a time when Catholic priests were ignorant of modern inventions, electronics, atomic energy, the hydrogen bomb, the latest discoveries of physical science and anthropology. But that was the time when everybody was ignorant, because the discoveries had not yet been made. In such an assumption about priests, Childs seems to be reading history backwards.

[72] Victor Riesel and Aaron Levenstein, "Labor Priests," *Look Magazine*, XIII (March 1, 1949), 35–39.

The greatest weakness that progressives find in traditional education is its authoritarianism. If the young are to acquire beliefs, our author maintains that they must be given the opportunity to inquire into the grounds for those beliefs. Yet he himself proposes for belief some ideas which he defines in a way that is both arbitrary and authoritarian.

> For an idea to be true, it must be valid in both of these aspects; it must define an act that can be carried out, and it must also define a condition that actually will come into existence when the prescribed action is carried out. . . . Truth denotes accurate prediction. . . .[73] Our acts are *free*, not simply because they are not under constraint from others, but because they are becoming *intelligent* . . . we become free as we *learn to think*.[74] . . . It is choice among significant life alternatives that is the essence of the *moral* act.[75]

There is no doubt that in specialized fields, words are often used in a specialized sense. An expert in such a field has a right to define his terms clearly. However, there is no justification for changing the meaning of such fundamental words as "true," "free," "moral"; nor has Childs offered any evidence by "operational procedure" or "public methods" which would convince us that these words have the meanings he at-

[73] Childs, *op. cit.*, p. 165.
[74] *Ibid.*, p. 151.
[75] *Ibid.*, p. 8; cf. also p. 20.

tributes to them. Furthermore, his changing of the meanings is not scientific; a specialized meaning is given to words in order to give greater clarity to ideas. If education is to be a democratic procedure in a democratic society, a procedure in which not only parents but also children are to be supremely active, especially with regard to policies, then parents will surely be confused when they read of moral aims or consequences and find education to be moral because schools are "organized and maintained by adults, and not by the children who attend them";[76] children will be confused when they find that "true" and "free" have a meaning for their educators different from the naive interpretation of their parents and companions. Such would be the result stemming from Childs' definitions; we should recall that elsewhere he extolled the naive approach and believes meanings to be primarily group possessions.

In his method of expounding the progressive philosophy, Childs has shown a certain consistency, though not of a very commendable kind. We find it in his continued reliance on hypotheses, on suppositions. Even in scientific investigation of the physical universe, such unverified suppositions do not spring unbidden into the scientist's mind. He believes they may be verifiable but when evidence shows them false or unverifiable, they are rejected. We would like to see Childs go through the process of verifying the suppositions he makes about the Catholic Church, its

[76] *Ibid.*, p. 6.

philosophy and educational system. We would ask him to reject those which the available evidence overthrows. We would be afraid to ask him to weigh the evidence *he* finds, because in so far as he has revealed them in *Education and Morals*, his powers of search are not very far-reaching. The evidence, however, is available to the scientific and methodical investigator.

3

At the danger of unduly lengthening this chapter, we would like to introduce another study which gives even more attention to the moral aspect of education. It is a work of collaboration and its thesis is something new from authors who subscribe mainly to progressive philosophy. It is a reaction to the adoration of scientific method as the be-all and end-all of matters intellectual and educational. The authors state their chief thought in no uncertain terms.

> But we hasten to insist that the prevailing custom of conceiving and running the educational program in an amoral atmosphere of pseudo-neutrality and in a normatively indifferent fragmentation of human understandings serves exactly to defeat the discipline of the most important functions of man's intelligence. It literally prevents the cultivation of wisdom in private and public decisions, choices, policy-making and planning—the heart of the democratic process.[77]

[77] Bruce R. Raup, George E. Axtelle, Kenneth D. Benne, B. Othanel Smith, *The Improvement of Practical Intelligence: The*

Frequently in the course of their work, these writers will condemn such neutrality;[78] they look askance at the poor preparation for practical affairs that is given to Americans;[79] we might note that among these Americans, there are educators. It is particularly interesting to note this inclusion of educators among the inept in moral matters;[80] perhaps in no other sphere have educators more constantly pontificated during recent years than in moral affairs. The problem which the authors have undertaken to study is one that Catholic educators put at the center of their philosophy; on the answer to that problem is built the theory and practice of Catholic education. For Raup and his co-authors, the introduction of a moral atmosphere in place of pseudo-neutrality is the beating of the "heart of the democratic process."

It is discouraging for us to find out what these thinkers mean by the democratic process, the ideal to be aimed at by both individuals and society as their life goal. It seems to be no more than a method. In fact, the authors point out that they are seeking a methodology. They have focused their attention in this way largely because methodology was instituted for informative knowledge but was neglected in the sphere of normative knowledge. For them, then, the essential feature in democracy is a community of per-

---

Central Task of Education (New York: Harper & Brothers, Publishers, 1950), p. 273.

[78] *Ibid.*, p. 63; cf. also p. 67.

[79] *Ibid.*, pp. 268, 271.

[80] *Ibid.*, p. 269.

suasion, decisions arrived at by the vote of the greatest number. This is an excellent way of arriving at decisions for practice; in political and social life it is often the only way; undoubtedly it is the basis of a democratically organized government which seems best to insure respect for man's individual personal worth. But it supposes foundations and the authors are not unaware of these presuppositions.

> The efforts at democratic administration and supervision will end in failure just as long as the moral foundations of democracy are not understood and the rationale of the democratic method remains obscure.[81]

There must be a common social-moral orientation;[82] convictions are necessary;[83] it is desirable to study the varying though often similar moral systems.[84] With all these statements we can readily agree. We find, however, that they cannot mean the same to the writers as to us.

> Even more basic than what people come to believe are the methods by which they arrive at these beliefs. . . . One of the most basic communities of persuasion a people can have is the method, including its sustaining ethical foundations, by which they attack their common problems.[85]

[81] *Ibid.*, p. 67.
[82] *Ibid.*, p. 281.
[83] *Ibid.*, p. 257.
[84] *Ibid.*, p. 281.
[85] *Ibid.*, p. 237.

A substantial section of the book under consideration is devoted to the value of symbols, the meaning of
words. Hence we feel extra justification for analyzing
and criticizing statements like those in the preceding
quotation. If the method of arriving at beliefs is the
most basic thing, how can any principles of ethics be
its sustaining foundation? "Sustaining foundation" is
the same as "basis." A method cannot be the last
foundation and at the same time be itself built on a
foundation. The authors make another statement
which seems to throw light on what ethics and
morality mean to them. In speaking of the value of
educational systems, they declare that the personal
commitment of the individual is imperative for the
integration of character; this commitment, we learn,
is to "a course of action, where social-moral consequences are confronted as imminent and inevi-
table. . . ." [86] The statement we call in question is the
following:

> Another characteristic of the situation we seek
> is that the personal commitment of the learner
> would be *imperative* within it. Whether the
> design he works out is good or bad, some design
> he should *have to* work out.[87]

The emphasis here is on the authors' italicized words;
the reader is thus apt to give less attention to the ideas
of "good" and "bad"; yet according to what "com-

[86] *Ibid.*, p. 270.
[87] *Ibid.*

mitment" seems to indicate, the design in question will have moral implications and the authors do not seem to care whether the solution is good or bad. If effectiveness or ineffectiveness is what is really meant rather than the moral good or bad, our criticism still stands, because according to these thinkers the criterion of *rightness* of a judgment is its effectiveness toward community persuasion.[88] It is always possible that one of these bad designs will be accepted by the mass of the people. Hence the morality advocated by this book is of a very questionable kind.

The collaborating authors single out a concept that has been the cause of much confusion in many discussions. That concept is the psychological effect of words. They recognize that some words bring more than a meaning with them; they set up an attitude or call forth a bias. The examples provided clearly show what is meant—Negro, fascism, democracy. In the course of their own investigation, however, an attitude can be detected, an attitude common to thinkers of the pragmatist school. They dislike absolute truth and fixed standards; they do not disprove them. They merely dislike them and then dismiss them as unworthy of a democratic people. If they consider them at all, they couple them so much with words that "bear such a freight of attitude and disposition on the part of those who use them"[89] that the reader will dismiss the possibility of such ideas or standards having any

[88] *Ibid.*, p. 205.
[89] *Ibid.*, p. 126.

basis. We find these ideas coupled, in other works, with words or phrases like "traditional," "indoctrination," "lack of consideration of alternatives." The writers of the present work have gone even farther.

> But there is still another pathological condition of this mood that is especially destructive of integrity. . . . It is fixity and stubborn oneness in devotion to an ideal or purpose or policy. Only one way is considered right. All else is wrong. This is often a resort of those who are most conscientious.[90]

Catholics in their millions are addicted to fixed standards and absolute truths; with them are many others, Americans as well as persons of other nationalities. Dismiss their views in trying to achieve that "democratic community of persuasion"; they are all pathological cases! We do not think that we overstretch the thought of the authors in drawing this conclusion. But there is something further. Consider the freight of attitude in the above quotation. Fixity is stubborn oneness; to most people stubbornness implies an unreasonable attitude. Again, one way is considered right; any other way is wrong. The authors do not make it clear that other ways are considered, that they are not automatically rejected without consideration. These thinkers do not make it clear that with fixity there can be change. They are aware of this fact, none the less, and when it suits their argument they present this truth in another way.

[90] *Ibid.*, p. 256.

There is an identity amid change, a persistent general amid varied particulars. . . .[91] We know as well as do all those who loudly contend so, that ends, ideals, generalized goals without means, without any definition, are vicious. . . .[92] Without the generalizations that transcend definite and particular operations, it is doubtful whether a people could continue long to be a people.[93]

One other point of criticism we make on this question of the psychological effect of words. We note that the authors tell us that fixity is often the resort of the most conscientious. Now, leadership is essential in a democracy; what separates the leader from the dictator (be he a Hitler or a city political boss) is integrity and devotion to the common good.[94] For the immature the teacher is a leader who "must make decisions and chart policies" that the children do not yet understand.[95] But apparently we dare not trust children to the most conscientious teachers. We must, according to Raup and his associates, be content with the less conscientious because the others are more likely to resort to fixity in truth and ideals. This conclusion is not specifically drawn by the authors; many readers will not take note of the contradiction; yet it is such contradictions which point to a faulty foundation in the basic philosophy of these writers.

[91] *Ibid.*, p. 197.
[92] *Ibid.*
[93] *Ibid.*, p. 195.
[94] *Ibid.*, p. 33.
[95] *Ibid.*

Natural law or natural rights have no meaning for the champions of the new moral atmosphere in education. They could find no satisfactory evidence for the existence of natural law or natural rights. Therefore they are constrained to reject any argument based on their existence.[96] The beliefs and customs of peoples are the origin of those "general normatives" [97] (note the avoidance of the word "laws") without which man cannot achieve organized society. It is interesting to note that the authors do not present the evidence they considered unsatisfactory as proof of the existence of natural law. They do, however, recognize that the individual has duties; they avoid mention of this word and present us with concepts like "imperatives" or with italicized "shoulds." In their educational scheme, character is important though at times it seems to denote nothing more than the interaction of organism and environment. The responsibility of schools with regard to character is, not to impose it, but to help students to organize their characters for the greatest development.[98] Their ideal must ever be the democratic community of persuasion.

As a conclusion, some further criticism of the work under discussion may be presented in a general way. The whole question of morality is treated without reference to God, although the authors give an occasional nod of recognition to Christianity. The demo-

[96] *Ibid.,* p. 81.
[97] *Ibid.,* p. 197.
[98] *Ibid.,* p. 236.

cratic process is the leading basic assumption on which the improvement of practical intelligence is to be built. No doubt the authors would agree in saying that respect for the individual is the cornerstone of democracy.[99] Yet the development of their argument seems, in a great way, to undermine the value of the individual. So much emphasis is given to the community of persuasion that the reader may lose sight of the practical meaning of this phrase (and is it not practical intelligence which is being considered?). It does not mean that every man's opinion is counted even in the fields in which he is expert. It does not mean that every man helps to make decisions. The opinions that count are of those who are in the majority; decisions are made by the greatest number. The opinions of a strong minority may help in some cases to modify decisions; yet so far as that minority is concerned such a course of action is only a compromise and our authors profess that compromise is not an ideal to aim at.[100] If the majority decides that an individual over three score years and ten has passed the stage of usefulness to society and should be liquidated, it is hard to see how respect for the individual would be basic in such a decision. The reply may be given that the objectives of our culture would prevent such a course. The answer will be valid only if our culture is based on something more solid than majority decisions.

[99] *Ibid.*, p. 205.
[100] *Ibid.*, p. 104.

The authors started the reader off with high hopes that, in the maelstrom of conflicting opinions, some indication would be given of where to turn for safe guidance. The answer given is not satisfactory. We have pointed out some of its weaknesses and inconsistencies; the authors themselves admit that they can offer no panacea.[101] Perhaps they would do well to ponder an assumption that underlies their words in the following quotation:

> Where shall we turn for principles and guides to action and decision, when, although old guides are failing us, we still must decide and act responsibly, and, if possible, intelligently? [102]

We would say that, at least in our century, some old guides have for the most part never been tried—those old guides, ten in number and known as the Ten Commandments.

[101] *Ibid.*, p. 267.
[102] *Ibid.*, p. 6.

Chapter Four . . . HOOK AND KALLEN: SPOKESMEN OF PREJUDICE

It is interesting to Catholics to find authors like Sidney Hook and Horace Kallen referring here and there in their writings to such familiar figures as St. Augustine, St. Thomas, the Thomists, or quoting from such sources as encyclical letters of the Popes. We watch these passages carefully to see what impression has been made on experimental minds by the thought of people who stand at the front lines in our school of philosophy. The two progressives we mention are men committed in loyalty to John Dewey and experimentalism. Hook's varied writings (some in collaboration with Kallen) and Kallen's long experience at Harvard and Columbia, on various important committees and in editorial positions, give evidence of veteran service in the progressive cause.

These men provide Catholic readers with evidence of having consulted Catholic sources. Naturally, we scrutinize the arguments deduced from such consultation. We expect them to misunderstand or underrate the arguments, say, of Aquinas, or to misjudge the statements of the Popes. If they did not, they would be Catholic in thought and not progressive. We do often find that they use references in one place to bolster up their argument and omit other references which would weaken their case. A separate consideration of their writing will show whether the title of this chapter is justified.

1

We shall begin with Hook. The conduct we have described is contrary to his principles, as it must be contrary to the principles of anyone who claims to be scientifically intellectual. Yet, as Hook says, there has always been a great difference between the talk about critical method and the practice of it.[1] His principle we quote; his practice we shall reveal by a study of his *Education for Modern Man*.

> The most obvious sign of indoctrination, as of propaganda which professes to reach conclusions by argument, is not outright invention but suppression of evidence that tends to invalidate or weaken a favored conclusion.[2]

By indoctrination Hook means the teaching and acceptance of beliefs through unrational or irrational means. We claim that Hook has suppressed evidence of which he must have been aware. For example, he lays down the best rule for the teacher of controversial subjects, declaring that he should build up the argument for the position *he* cannot accept. Anyone with a slight knowledge of the works of St. Thomas Aquinas could hardly fail to notice that this is the

---

[1] Reprinted from *Education for Modern Man* by Sidney Hook (copyright, 1946, by Sidney Hook), p. 113. Used by permission of The Dial Press, Inc.

[2] *Ibid.*, p. 123.

mode which he follows. Hook makes no mention of this method of Aquinas though he remarks that there is no one who would not like to go to school to Plato, Aquinas, Newton or Darwin.[3] An omission of this kind seems to constitute suppression of evidence, especially when noted in conjunction with a footnote that appears in Hook's work. Our author there maintains that orthodox Thomists do not want the truths of faith critically examined.[4]

Outright invention also finds its place in Hook's evaluation of the metaphysical outlook on man's nature. He claims that those who hold for metaphysics (Jacques Maritain and Fulton Sheen as well as Robert Hutchins and Mortimer Adler) would limit education to reason alone, ignoring man's emotional and sense structure. Hook fails to see the patent fallacy of confusing essential and accidental (terms used in their philosophical connotation) differences between men and animals. In this particular section, he goes blithely along condemning supposedly metaphysical principles concerning man's nature which, in reality, are no more than Hook's mistaken ideas of what men like Jacques Maritain teach.[5] Our author has recourse to invention when he treats of the Christian teaching on the relationship of soul and body. Hook rejects the idea of the soul destined to dwell in the body and the consequent emphasis on education for the soul to the

[3] *Ibid.*, p. 222.
[4] *Ibid.*, p. 210.
[5] *Ibid.*, chapter II.

exclusion of the body and its needs.) We agree with his rejection here; Catholics deny that the soul dwells in the body in such a way. In fact, the analogy of dwelling, though sometimes used, does no justice to the Catholic teaching. Soul and body form one individual person; there is no mere loose union of two parts, one material, the other spiritual. There is one indivisible person.

Our author declares that we owe him a proof that a supernatural soul exists. First of all, he confuses spiritual and supernatural. Catholics do not believe their souls to be essentially supernatural. They are natural but spiritual. Secondly, experimental evidence for the existence of this spiritual soul has been offered; Hook's denial shows unabashed voluntary blindness. If he had consulted any book of Catholic philosophy dealing with this question, he could have found the evidence. How do scientists know that electricity exists? While no one knows what exactly it is, they know something of the nature of it. They know it is not water; if by what electricity does and water cannot do people can recognize differences, so the argument from activity is valid in distinguishing the spiritual soul from the body. The soul is not matter because it can do what matter alone cannot do. Why should such an argument be valid in one case and not in the other?

In this particular section of his study, still another error casts doubt on the sincerity of our author. Here is the quotation:

> In fact, the achievements of genuine knowledge about human nature in medicine, biology, psychology and history have been largely won by a bitter struggle against obstacles set in the path of scientific inquiry by believers in a supernatural soul.[6]

We have already pointed out the wrong use of the word "supernatural." We can easily detect an additional error caused by the author's neglect of his own principles. He gives no proof of the obstacles he mentions. Furthermore, history in general and the history of scientists in particular will show that the greatest number of outstanding scientists believed in God and an immortal soul. What makes Hook's error the more flagrant is the fact that, but a few lines before this quotation, he spoke of the need for proof and experimental evidence. We ask Hook to make a list of scientists (like Pasteur, Fabre, Alexis Carrel) who believed in God and place it side by side with a list of those who were atheists. Then we shall see the value of his assertions.

Our author has written his book on the principles of progressive education in a free society for free men. It is important, even in his philosophy, that people learn to recognize evidence for what it is worth. We expect from him an application of the ability to sift evidence. To appeal to uncritical acceptance of a belief is not sufficient grounds for drawing a conclusion. He has done just this.

[6] *Ibid.*, p. 21.

> The deepest traditions of a community are those that are so completely taken for granted that they rarely emerge on the level of critical awareness and still more rarely become subjects of debate. . . .[7]

In the community in which he seems to have placed himself by his uncritical procedure, viz., the community of pseudoscholars, false scientists and quasi-experts, there is an assumption that religion is and has been opposed to science and must naturally be so. Hook appeals to that emotional assumption and seems to think that he is not bound to offer proof. He should have pointed out the specific instances where blocking of scientific inquiry took place through people who believed in the existence of the soul. Then, to be truly scientific method, his procedure should have been to point out also the instances where scientific inquiry was advanced by people believing in the existence of the soul. In the face of such evidence, the fair-minded reader would be enabled to draw his own conclusion. If Hook felt that all this would require too much detail for the scope of his work, he should have omitted his reference to the matter.

Misrepresentation is also to be found in the work we are criticizing. Its author maintains that theological and moral beliefs are taught by traditionalists and religious teachers in such a way as to provoke no discussions or allow no questions. His language is clear:

> But a *critical* evaluation of dogmas is precisely

[7] *Ibid.*, p. 84.

what those who urge the prescription of religious and theological study do *not* want.[8]

In a free and democratic society, there are two closely linked and important rights guaranteed to the individual. They are the right to a fair trial and belief in a man's innocence until he has been proved guilty. It is true that even in the United States a jury may be packed or a judge may be corrupt; it is true that emotions may run high and a prisoner may be treated as guilty before proof of guilt has been established. Yet these aberrations are deplored by the fair-minded citizen. How, then, do we expect a group of just and intelligent readers to react when an accusation is made against any individual or group in the field of philosophy? Will they believe the accusation without proof? We hardly think so. Hence, we call attention to the accusation made by Hook.

The Catholic position is briefly this. The accusation is unfounded. However, the good name of an innocent accused usually suffers some stigma from the accusation. He is forced, even though unfairly, to offer some defense. The defense we offer is a matter of simple scientific inquiry. We ask any reader, even Hook, to consult any professional text-book of Catholic dogmatic theology; such inquiry will reveal that the method of study entails a close examination of the doctrines we call heresies and a consideration of the proofs that are offered to sustain those beliefs.

[8] *Ibid.*, p. 109.

We find an amazing statement by our author on this question of teaching religion.

> By their [that is, teachers of religion] own admission they propose to offer, literally, courses in apologetics.[9]

The context in which these words occur seems to indicate that in Hook's mind there is nothing so ridiculous or shameless as to teach apologetics. We suspect that our author did not even consult an English dictionary to find out the meaning of the word. It finds its root in a Greek verb which signifies "to give a full account of" or "to give reasons for." [10] In Catholic circles, apologetics means the giving of the rational proofs for the divine authority of the Catholic Church.[11] It is surely not a lack in scientific method for Catholics to investigate the questions of whether God exists and whether the Church is nothing more than a man-made institution. Our author may think that the Church has no authority; he may think that there is no God or that, if God does exist, His existence makes no difference to us men. If, however, an author knows enough to introduce the concept of apologetics into his writing, we are entitled to expect from him an understanding of what apologetics means. If he condemns without understanding, he shows

[9] *Ibid.*, p. 110.
[10] Liddell and Hart, *Greek-English Lexicon.*
[11] M. Sheehan, *Apologetics and Catholic Doctrine* (Dublin: M. H. Gill & Son, Ltd., 1942), Part I, p. 1.

himself unscholarly; if he misrepresents, he shows himself unobjective and prejudiced.

Divine authority is an idea on which Hook has hostile feelings and he looks to the day when "the authority of method has replaced the authority of creed. . . ." [12] His general principle demands that truths be accepted only when they have been evaluated critically. Catholics, on the other hand, teach children to practice religion and believe the truths of religion long before such pupils can pass judgment on the credibility of the doctrine; they believe on the authority of the Church or their parents or their teachers. This procedure seems to be completely contrary to experimental principles. But what is experimental procedure? Let Hook again speak:

> But the school cannot begin at too early an age to strengthen the child's powers of intelligence and to develop habits of reasonableness, even if on some crucial matters, it must supplement them with other methods of suasion until he reaches maturity and can rationally test these matters for himself. . . .[13] but until full maturity is reached they cannot assume total responsibility for the decision as to what constitutes their educational needs. . . .[14] The practice of democracy comes first in the order of time; the justification of democracy comes first in the order of logic.[15]

[12] Hook, *op. cit.*, p. 137.
[13] *Ibid.*, pp. 106–107.
[14] *Ibid.*, p. 146.
[15] *Ibid.*, p. 119.

Catholics could not ask for a better statement of principles to justify their teaching of religious doctrine and practice to children. The practice of religion comes first in the order of time. Such priority cannot be right for democracy and wrong for religion. No doubt children have little appreciation of Hook's distinction between the authority of method and the authority of creed. In fact, the other manners of suasion used by the experimentalists may perhaps rest, not on the authority of method, but on the authority of experimentalists. Even our author suspects the authority of scientists.

> We do not need to wait for the results of experiments on transference of training to realize that a great many able scientists who pontificate on matters outside their fields display not only ignorance but utter inability to grasp essential points at issue or to make valid elementary inferences.[16]

As a concluding indication of the incomplete and one-sided interpretation of the religious question and education as presented by Sidney Hook, we introduce the problem of juvenile delinquency and crime.

> Whoever holds the opinion that religious education is either a necessary or sufficient condition for the prevention of crime does so in defiance of available statistics on the subject.[17]

[16] *Ibid.*, p. 95.
[17] *Ibid.*, p. 109.

We can immediately concede that religious education is not a sufficient condition for the prevention of crime. Other environmental factors are involved. Hook mentions available statistics; he gives no reference nor quotation; we are presumably supposed to take the authority of method as sufficient guarantee. However, it would do no injustice to his line of thought if we were to conclude from his statements that the ineffectiveness of religious education as a preventative of delinquency is clearly demonstrated by available statistics. Experts in the field of criminology find themselves unable to draw such a conclusion. There are too many other factors involved. Even where the numbers might indicate a larger percentage of Catholics among criminals, in certain areas, than of other religious affiliations, Gillin points out that the studies on which the figures are based reveal that the Catholics concerned are from the poorest part of the population.[18] Hence, along with religious loyalty, other social and environmental factors must be considered. Other experts, too, show that it is not scientific to draw such a conclusion from these religious statistics of criminals.[19]

We would also suggest that some attention be paid

[18] John Lewis Gillin, *Criminology and Penology* (Third edition; New York: D. Appleton-Century Co., 1945), p. 207.

[19] Walter C. Reckless and Mapheus Smith, *Juvenile Delinquency* (New York: McGraw Hill Book Co., Inc., 1932), p. 151. Cf. also William Healy and Augustine Bronner, *New Light on Delinquency and its Treatment* (Yale University Press, 1936), pp. 70–71.

to the frequent utterances of J. Edgar Hoover on the question of juvenile delinquency. He has stressed the importance of religion as a factor in helping toward the solution of this problem. We feel sure that, as Director of the Federal Bureau of Investigation whose statistics are the measuring rod for the extent of crime in the United States, Hoover is in a better position than Sidney Hook to pontificate on the question of juvenile delinquency.

2

A similar pattern of uncritical method is displayed in the essay of Horace M. Kallen. Here it is possibly more outright and obvious. This author takes note of the Catholic school system and quotes from papal documents. He does not confine himself to matters educational but treats (and, for the most part, treats very well) of many social problems facing modern society, problems which will, according to him, find their solution only in a school system that befits a democracy. Before seeing how Kallen presents the Catholic viewpoint, we propose some of his ideas that bear directly on education and the educand.

> In every culture, the task of education is to realize the ideal of manhood it cherishes, its ideal and no other. . . .[20] Modern democracy does not establish the school to teach a grammar

[20] Reprinted from *The Education of Free Men: An Essay Toward a Philosophy of Education for Americans* by Horace M. Kallen (copyright, 1949, by Horace M. Kallen), p. x. Used by permission of Farrar, Straus and Young, Inc., Publishers.

of assent, but to impart an art of enquiry and judgment. . . .[21] In a very obvious sense there is no education that is not historical education.[22]

The children to be educated are people but they are not born with personality;[23] this is what education gives them. At birth they are only animals; they are raised to a higher level by a process of acculturation.[24] They proceed by free and deliberate choice to what is new;[25] there is no fixed place for people in the world but they "move from one to the other as their hearts prompt and their powers carry." [26] These are some of the ideas expounded by Kallen in his philosophy of education.

For our author, the great importance of democratic society is that it is free. Kallen, on Condorcet's authority, seems to hold that truth is a necessity in free society. He does not say what truth is but he leaves no doubt as to what it is not; there can be no authority as basis for truth nor may it be considered an absolute.

> . . . "liberty would be in the greatest of dangers" if a government, any more than a church, had the smallest influence over the art of discovering and transmitting truth and could fix a

[21] *Ibid.*, pp. 84–85.
[22] *Ibid.*, p. 104.
[23] *Ibid.*, p. 172.
[24] *Ibid.*, p. 259.
[25] *Ibid.*, p. 129.
[26] *Ibid.*, p. 169.

body of doctrine and impose a discipline. This
art is peculiar to education.[27]

By "education" the author really means educators; he
does not seem to be aware that he is claiming a monopoly for a small body of men, many of whom show
themselves ill versed in the art of discovering truth.
According to Kallen, the only means of overcoming
the poverty of ignorance is by way of the public
school system.[28] That such a system must, of its very
nature, be influenced in no small way by local or
state government does not seem to present a flaw to
his argumentation.

The Catholic parochial school system receives a
great deal of attention from our author; he is not
merely critical but obviously hostile to things Catholic. He finds it annoying that released time should be
permitted for religious instruction since, according to
him, the scientific study of religion is taboo.[29] Free
inquiry, consideration of alternatives, the scientific
approach, such are some of the prime factors in true
education. From an author demanding these things
one would rightly expect a knowledge of what he
condemns, data and argument to back up his criticism,
and a presentation without distortion of his opponents'
point of view. It is a vain quest to look for such hall-
marks of science and objectivity in Kallen's presentation of Catholic aims and teaching.

[27] *Ibid.*, p. 133.
[28] *Ibid.*
[29] *Ibid.*, p. 145.

His interpretation of one part of Christian teaching is that man was wholly corrupt in original sin, a corruption which could be amended only by the "miracle of grace" that demanded as a prerequisite an act of faith in defiance of reason, a faith which saved only because it was belief in the impossible in nature and the absurd in reason.[30] Catholics will oppose a system of education or society based on these premises; they will not accept Kallen's assertion that they are the doctrines which Catholics are bound to believe.[31] Again, according to our author, there was no aiming at educational freedom until John Dewey arrived on the scene; even after the First World War, Catholic education brought new life to the totalitarianism of authority. Hence, traditionalists could bring into the first ranks of their army, not only Plato, Aristotle and Thomas Aquinas, but also Hitler, Mussolini and Stalin.[32]

The Papal Sacerdotal State (presumably the whole one hundred and eight acres of it) is one of the four outstanding totalitarian powers, according to Kallen.[33] It is strange that scientists and research students from any part of the world have been invited into the very heart of that State, to work and study among the wealth of material in the Vatican Library Archives. However, Kallen's insinuations will have their effect on the reader who is not equipped with the back-

[30] *Ibid.*, p. xi.
[31] *Ibid.*, p. xiv.
[32] *Ibid.*, p. 7.
[33] *Ibid.*, p. 185.

ground knowledge to judge whether our author is giving historical fact or emotional fancy in his estimate of the Church. We do not blame readers for distrusting or even hating Catholics if their only source of information about the Catholic Church is such writing as we are at present considering. We do hope that the fair-minded reader will be prepared to check from primary sources the truth or falsehood of the many accusations levelled against us. Intellectual honesty and the American democratic way clearly point out such a course of inquiry.

We wish, then, to indicate some of the places where Kallen has distorted the evidence or has failed to give evidence. For example, he has indulged his fancy in explaining the change in a teacher from a lively young college graduate to schoolmarm, the latter being a sort of sexless dehumanized being without understanding of life or hope of marriage and lacking the mentality suitable for training the young. This, Kallen tells us, is due in no small way to the celibacy of the Catholic clergy and the Catholic sisters who are engaged in educative work.[34] Even in the present public school life, this sinister influence comes to bear on the teacher and marks her out for old-maidhood. Kallen has no evidence for this but, after all, *he* thinks it is a good explanation. What next! With such a scientifically backed explanation will the intelligent reader be satisfied?

The American people may be led to question

[34] *Ibid.*, p. 48.

whether the schools are giving them what they want. Kallen maintains that they are doing as good a job as ever was done.

> However, the record contains nothing to warrant a contention that some other institution, such as the church, can do better than the school in the education of free men. Indeed, the record does contain many things to warrant the contention that they have done and are doing worse; and would do still worse without the schools to measure by.[35]

Beyond the vague general term "many things," Kallen gives no more than this veiled accusation. Free inquiry, scientific method! In a footnote to page 73, he gives some statistics on parochial schools which, he says, form seventy-nine per cent of the nation's private schools. In this seventy-nine per cent, they "indoctrinate, if they do not educate, ninety-two per cent of their 2,611,000 students." A similar insinuation is contained in a footnote to page 47. There he refers to the sisters who teach in Catholic schools almost without salary.

> Their inexpensive services enable the parochial schools to offer the lowest-cost schooling which the nation knows, with corresponding values in the comparative result.[36]

[35] *Ibid.*, p. 35.
[36] *Ibid.*, p. 47.

108

It would be strange if the Catholic schools were not criticized, but the criticism should be scientific. Kallen notes that progressive schools were justly criticized because of many absurd extremes to which some carried what they thought to be Dewey's doctrine. He takes care to quote a study made to show the superiority of progressive pupils.[37] When it comes to Catholic schools, however, it is sufficient to state that they are inefficient, that they are giving inferior education; there is no need of proof, no need of proceeding according to scientific method.

We have stated that Kallen cites the encyclicals of Popes and other Catholic sources. There are certain guiding principles in the use of quotations. They must not be wrenched from their context and applied in a way contrary to their author's meaning. It is easy to give examples of Kallen's use of quotations which will show a complete lack of understanding of the meaning in the original context. Here is one instance:

> "As a mandate to teach, Christ conferred infallibility in educative work on his church." [38]

These words are taken by Kallen from Pius XI's *Letter on the Christian Education of Youth*. From them, our author implies that there is no room in Catholic schools for modern science since there can be no deviation from unchangeable Catholic teaching. It would be too much to expect him to notice that the

[37] *Ibid.*, p. 266.
[38] *Ibid.*, p. 191.

whole context of this quotation deals with Christ's doctrine and commandments and has nothing to do with engineering or geometry or chemistry. Kallen's idea of papal infallibility, as revealed in the passages which immediately precede this quotation, shows a complete ignorance of what can be sufficiently well grasped by children not yet scientifically trained, namely, that the Pope is infallible only on matters of faith and morals in the very special circumstances when he is speaking and acting officially as head of the Church.

Our author offers another quotation, this time from Leo XIII, to show that there is no hope of Catholics being educated in freedom.

> "All Catholics must believe what the Pope says, especially as regards modern liberties.
>
> "As regards opinions, whatever the Roman Pontiffs have hitherto taught or shall hereafter teach, must be held with a firm grasp of the mind, and so often as the occasion requires, must be openly professed.
>
> "Especially with reference to the so-called 'liberties' which are greatly coveted these days, all must stand by the judgment of the Apostolic See, and have the same mind." [39]

Kallen avoids mention of the following information which he could have found in the same encyclical and some of it in the same context. He does not declare

[39] *Ibid.*, p. 191 (quoted from Leo XIII's *Immortale Dei*).

what the Pope meant by these so-called liberties,[40] nor does he quote Leo's words to show that there is no condemnation of any kind of government which the people care to choose,[41] that the Pope is not opposed to scientific research;[42] our author fails to state Leo's instruction that no one is to be forced to embrace the Catholic faith, that governments may tolerate false religions.[43] At this stage in his argument, Kallen takes exception to words of Monsignor John Ryan, which declare that error has not the same rights as truth.[44] Now, Kallen may disagree with Catholics as to what is true and what is not. But to maintain that it makes no difference to children whether they are taught truth or falsehood, as he apparently does, seems to demand the stifling of active intelligence.

Since Leo XIII is internationally known as the Pope of Labor, Kallen could have extended his acquaintance to Leo's encyclical on *The Condition of the Working Classes*. Our author has a good grasp of the ills which afflict economic society; if he had delved into Leo's writings on such social questions, he would have realized that the Pope also had a good understanding of these problems. The difficulty of child labor is a matter which Kallen considers. He takes time to interject a remark that opposition to the Child Labor

[40] Pope Leo XIII, *The Pope and the People: Select Letters and Addresses on Social Questions* (London: Catholic Truth Society, 1903), p. 87.

[41] *Ibid.*, p. 91.

[42] *Ibid.*, p. 93.

[43] *Ibid.*, p. 91.

[44] Kallen, *op. cit.*, p. 191.

Amendment came, significantly enough, from "those religious establishments whose ideals are most traditional, fundamentalist and authoritarian."[45] Since these epithets are commonly used by Kallen of the Catholic Church, and since there was some Catholic opposition to this unadopted amendment, how can we justify ourselves? We do so merely by indicating once more Kallen's unscientific, unobjective presentation. Catholic opposition arose, not because Catholics approved the injustice and inhumanity of child labor practices, but because the wording of the amendment seemed to give totalitarian power over children to the government, a development to be avoided at all costs in American democracy. Our author may disagree and consider Catholic fears groundless. If he has intellectual honesty that does not fear competition, he should have revealed the motives for Catholic opposition to the Child Labor Amendment.[46] Furthermore, Catholic opinion was divided on this question.

While prejudice seems to have guided Kallen in his presentation and interpretation of papal utterances, this is not the only scientific deficiency he has shown. He reveals a remarkable ignorance of Catholic doctrine and practice which he condemns so readily and so forcefully. Examples of this ignorance are to be found when he speaks of the Catholic rite of Confirmation,[47] the doctrine of papal infallibility (as

[45] *Ibid.*, p. 68.
[46] Raymond W. Murray and Frank T. Flynn, *Social Problems* (New York: F. S. Crofts & Co., 1947), p. 590.
[47] Kallen, *op. cit.*, p. 70.

112

already noted), when he believes the Church to teach that free will is bad will.[48] Further evidence of prejudice or ignorance is to be found in his reference to Pius XI's classification of the Church as a perfect society. On this point, Kallen makes no reference to the words of both Leo XIII [49] and Pius XI [50] to the effect that the state is also a perfect society.

The fellowship of scholars is valuable and leads to a community of interest and aim which even religious differences will not hinder. Admittance to this informal community should be based on the prerequisite of true scholarship which will never descend to the level of mob oratory and emotional catchwords. It is unfortunate that a chapter of such recrimination should have to be included in an appeal for a truer and more precise application of the scientific method. Yet evidence makes it clear that we cannot remain in an ivory tower built on the belief that everyone who writes writes with sincerity.

[48] *Ibid.*, p. 260.
[49] *Five Great Encyclicals*, p. 40.
[50] *Ibid.*, p. 51.

Chapter Five . . . BRAMELD: ADVOCATE OF RECONSTRUCTIONISM

The field of education has ever produced an abundant crop of "isms" and from New York University issue the writings of Theodore Brameld as the prophet of reconstructionism. This new philosophy is an offspring of progressivism to which it is still most closely allied. The reconstructionist, however, believes that progressivism, though good as far as it goes, does not go far enough. The very name of the new school of thought indicates that its followers aim to reconstruct a tottering culture. In Brameld, they have an able leader who does not fear to bring clearly to the fore valid objections against the progressive tenets.

While Brameld shows a keen mind for seeing the weaknesses to be found in modern democratic education, he does not display an equal power of synthesis. His proposals seem to lack the concreteness we are led to expect. We find, too, in the course of his writing, many unsupported assumptions about medieval philosophy and organized religion, many deficiencies in his treatment of vital questions like the nature of man, and not a few inconsistencies in his own definitions and principles. We shall, in accordance with the aim of our study, concentrate on such faults. At the same time, we are aware of the merit of a lot of the material to be found in Brameld's writings.

1

Two statements by our author provide a solid basis for scientific investigation.

> . . . this volume . . . insists on the most scrupulous consideration of all varieties of beliefs at odds with its own. . . .[1] On the contrary, we should consider as deliberately and fully as possible, the contributions and methods, on the one hand, of contemporary American schools and, on the other hand, of our most influential educational theories.[2]

Scrupulous consideration of any set of beliefs is guided by several principles. We have no doubt that Brameld will concede the validity of these principles. First, the beliefs in question should be stated clearly and the reasons for their rejection should be proposed. Unfounded assumptions are not enough. Secondly, an author should avoid the use of words loaded with insinuation. Brameld seems to sin in both respects.

> Organized religion, as we have known it, is authoritarian; it claims a monopoly on absolute truths and values which presumably entitles it to impose these dogmas upon everyone it can reach.[3]

Let us for the moment by-pass the question of authori-

---

[1] Theodore Brameld, *Ends and Means in Education: A Mid-century Appraisal* (First edition; New York: Harper & Brothers, 1950), p. 84.

[2] *Ibid.*, p. 221.

[3] *Ibid.*, p. 83.

tarianism. The second part of the passage just quoted is completely incorrect, and very little investigation will reveal it so. Organized religion does not claim a monopoly of absolute truths and values. To begin with, the term "organized religion" embraces the many forms of Protestantism and the Catholic Church. The Catholic Church claims that she alone possesses the whole truth taught by Christ whereby the world can reach eternal salvation; she also claims infallibility in teaching that truth. No Protestant sect lays claim to any sort of infallibility. Furthermore, the claim of the Catholic Church does not include all absolute truths. Neither does it impose such truths as are in its keeping on anyone outside the Catholic Church. Reference to the Church's Canon Law on this matter would have saved Brameld from making unscientific and untrue statements.

Non-Catholic children will not be baptized in the Catholic Church unless at least one parent consents; neither will an adult be received into the Church unless knowingly, willingly and with proper instruction. That is to say, he must see that belief rests on reasonable grounds; he must recognize that the truths contain nothing contrary to reason; he must be convinced in his own mind that the beliefs proposed by the Catholic Church should be believed. Such a consent is entirely in keeping with Brameld's teaching. He tells us that a conviction is nothing less than a reasoned conclusion.[4] Reason will bring any honest

[4] *Ibid.*, p. 149.

investigator as far in the Catholic faith as we have pointed out.

Our author uses words that are lacking in precision and are therefore misleading. Take, for example, the term "church" which he uses frequently. He says that the dogmas and rituals of the Church are the best means of propaganda for perennialism.[5] What does he mean by "the Church"? Is it the Catholic Church? If so, we would ask him to enlarge particularly on his reference to rituals; we shall ourselves give a more specific answer on the question of dogmas when we treat of indoctrination. Does he mean to include the Catholic Church and Protestantism? Do any of the Protestant sects claim to teach dogma? Do they all claim to indulge in ritual? Surely a generic term like "church" lacks the necessary precision when used in criticism of points of supposed belief or practice, points which cannot be verified in each and all of the organizations concerned. The author may object that we are quibbling, that everyone knows what is meant when a writer speaks of "the Church." However, in a scientific work let us be scientific. We can suggest a parallel which might be more telling. Suppose we accuse modern educators of indulging in methodological fads and losing sight of the fundamental questions of educational philosophy. Such an accusation is clearly unjust because the term "educators" is too general; it includes thinkers of many fairly well differentiated philosophies. No doubt some of these philos-

[5] *Ibid.*, p. 90.

ophers would rise in indignation to disclaim any part in such faddism; and they would be right. So, too, we object to the term "church" used in a vague generic way.

Another principle of guidance in the scrupulous consideration of opposing beliefs would be the full study of contemporary American schools and the most influential educational theories. Brameld proposed to undertake such a study. He tells us, however, that the three outstanding contemporary theories are progressivism, essentialism and perennialism.[6] The spokesman he chooses for the third is Mr. Robert M. Hutchins, formerly chancellor of the University of Chicago. In meeting the arguments of Hutchins, our author feels satisfied that he has scotched the snake of Thomism and even killed it. This is one example of the lacunae to be found in his work. We shall give it lengthier consideration in our criticism of his recent *Patterns of Educational Philosophy*. Brameld is not unaware of the value of Aristotle's and Thomas' works; he declares that a course in perennialism should concentrate on the writings of these two men. He should also be aware that great exponents of Aristotelean and Thomistic philosophy are to be found among Catholic priests. He should recognize, too, that a large percentage of contemporary American schools are Catholic schools—at all levels. Hence, in leaving Catholic philosophy out of his divisions, he is false to his principle of scrupulous consideration.

[6] *Ibid.*, p. 7.

One of the chapters of this work of Brameld's is devoted to the consideration of organized religion and education,[7] while there are numerous references throughout to traditional religion. The most important topic our author considers from the religious aspect is that of indoctrination. It will not be very difficult to show that he is neither consistent nor scientific in this matter. What he means by indoctrination is stated in the following quotation.

> In brief, it is that method of learning by communication which proceeds primarily in one direction (from the "communicator" to the "communicee") for the purpose of inculcating in the mind and behavior of the latter a firm acceptance of some one doctrine or systematic body of beliefs—a doctrine assumed in advance by its exponents to be so supremely true, so good, so beautiful as to justify no need for critical, scrupulous, thoroughgoing comparison with alternative doctrines.[8]

According to him, the Church has for centuries openly taught its beliefs in this way through its chief indoctrinators, that is, its priests.[9] Values which are thus taught on the assumption that alternatives are false and bad, do not rest on any solid basis.[10] Speaking of workers' education, Brameld refers back to his definition of indoctrination. He declares that to teach only

[7] *Ibid.*, chapter IX, pp. 80–85.
[8] *Ibid.*, p. 88.
[9] *Ibid.*
[10] *Ibid.*, p. 84.

one labor policy to the exclusion of others, even as matters for consideration, if not for practice, is nothing short of indoctrination—"(defined earlier as the attempt to inculcate one doctrine as absolutely true, by comparison with which all alternative doctrines are false). . . ." [11]

It is our contention that this second definition is different from that which the author has already given. The first definition of indoctrination was the true one, the second is false but it is the one which Brameld follows through his book when he condemns the practices of organized religion. The essential part of his original definition is omitted in the second instance. That essential part was that the beliefs indoctrinated were *assumed in advance* to be true so that there was *no need for critical consideration of alternatives*. Suppose the truths were not assumed in advance to be true but were proved to be true. Suppose the alternative doctrines were scrupulously considered and found to be false. In such case, what would Brameld call the teaching in question? His arguments and references show that he calls it indoctrination; his scientific definition shows that he should not call it such.

The truths which the Catholic Church proposes for belief are not logically assumed in advance to be true nor are they taught without solid consideration of alternatives. The Catholic Church claims to teach in a reasoned way and Brameld has not even tried to dis-

[11] *Ibid.*, p. 148.

prove that claim. The layout of text-books on dogmatic theology whereby its "chief indoctrinators," Catholic priests, are trained, proposes the contrary beliefs and teaching as they set out to prove each thesis. We do not, of course, expect children of eight years of age to learn by means of text-books on dogmatic theology. Brameld does not seem to have consulted such a book. Here we rightly begin to doubt the merits of that scrupulous attention to alternative beliefs which our author promised.

Brameld is sufficiently realistic to see that there is a great deal of authoritarianism in public education, not only in religious matters but especially in the economic and political fields.[12] His excuse for this is that the ideal has not yet been brought to reality. Yet even here, he is inconsistent. The frequent emphasis on "democracy," "popular majority," "the greatest possible consensus," expresses a devotion to the counting of heads, which practice involves him in contradiction.

> . . . the schools should be released from encrusted pedagogical routines and domination by any groups except popular majorities. . . .[13]
> . . . In fact, the minority may conceivably be right.[14]

Brameld's teaching seems to justify domination by a majority even though it is quite possible that the ma-

[12] *Ibid.*, p. 83.
[13] *Ibid.*, p. 38.
[14] *Ibid.*, p. 44.

jority may be wrong. Yet on the subject of indoctrination, our author advises against doing the wrong thing.

> We would be wiser to do nothing than to do the wrong things, at least until education is much farther along.[15]

Self-contradiction does not occur just once in this work of Brameld's. In speaking of values he claims that there should be some center of integration and suggests "self-realization" as the best value for that purpose. Education must face the problem of values even though there is difficulty in deciding the appropriate time for training in values.

> That a beginning should be made in the elementary school is obvious, for to inculcate the old ethical dogmas uncritically then is to make it well-nigh impossible for the secondary school to undo that inculcation later.[16]

A clear contradiction of this statement is to be found in another section of the book.

> In the earliest years, children must absorb some facts and rules by a degree of inculcation in order to get along with any group.[17]

Brameld even goes so far as to say that indoctrination may be necessary at times in high school and in col-

[15] *Ibid.*, p. 83.
[16] *Ibid.*, p. 45.
[17] *Ibid.*, p. 89.

lege. Such a thesis, he declares, is not a concession to indoctrination, since the frame of reference is education as a whole and not any part of it taken out of its context.[18] This is precisely the answer of Catholic educational philosophy when charged with indoctrinating children with religious truths before they can evaluate them. It is difficult to see why such an answer is valid when Brameld makes it for Brameld's philosophy but is considered irrelevant (and often not considered at all) when Catholics make it for Catholic doctrine. Surely this is a strange example of "most scrupulous consideration of all varieties of belief at odds with its own." [19]

Brameld agrees with progressives in their rejection of absolutes. Because of its fixed criteria, perennialism loses whatever intellectual appeal it might have had.

> Perennialism is dubious for a number of reasons, but especially because, in its central belief in the self-evidence of truth and values which are beyond public and scientific verification, it exposes itself to the grave accusation of setting up absolute criteria or fixed standards.[20]

Passing over his incorrect assumption on the nature of self-evidence, we direct attention to his criterion. He finds no more reliable test of truth or goodness "than that which the widest possible consensus of citizens

[18] *Ibid.*
[19] *Ibid.*, p. 84.
[20] *Ibid.*, p. 17; cf. also p. 236.

manages to fashion critically and openly together." [21]
At the same time, Brameld is not opposed to basic
beliefs.

> . . . many citizens in every walk of life are
> ready to agree that one of the most important,
> if not the single most important, of obligations
> confronting any human being is to clarify his
> basic beliefs. . . .[22] For every culture, includ-
> ing our own, has a pattern of basic beliefs—po-
> litical, economic, religious, moral, esthetic,
> scientific—which provides those who accept
> that culture with a sense of consistency and sig-
> nificance.[23]

Presumably the basic beliefs of Catholic culture are
to be rejected as being beyond scientific verification
or as being of no significance.

It is very easy to show that if anyone should accept
the basic beliefs of Catholic philosophy, that person is
our author. In the first place, his test of truth is the
widest possible consensus of citizens and he does not
limit this to citizenship of one country but extends it
on an international basis. Where else can he find a
greater consensus of truths and basic beliefs than
among Catholics of all nations? Perhaps it is unfair to
use this criterion when it favors traditional religion!
Secondly, Brameld aims to champion democracy with
its values, which, to him, provides the highest form of
society. Why do people accept these values? Is it

[21] *Ibid.*, p. 183; cf. also p. 44.
[22] *Ibid.*, p. 10.
[23] *Ibid.*, p. 222.

because of the public and scientific verification demanded by him from perennialism? It hardly seems
so, according to his own words.

> No one should deny, furthermore, that the
> values involved in the democratic program,
> while to a considerable extent subject to scien-
> tific analysis, are *ultimately* chosen or rejected
> because they seem to us to be *intrinsically* better
> or worse than alternative values. . . .[24] But the
> point is that, since these values flow from
> springs of nature of which each person is a part,
> each person must testify to their vitality and
> then, with others who so testify, arrive finally
> at mutual agreement that here indeed are the
> values which they share.[25]

The words "ultimately" and "intrinsically" are not
italicized in Brameld's text but they are the key words
in the quotation since they point to a criterion somewhat different from a majority vote. The author
alleges that the concept in the second section is not
that of a merely subjective or arbitrary certainty.
Once more we are presented with an example of inconsistency in Brameld's own philosophy.

2

In *Patterns of Educational Philosophy*, Professor
Brameld undertakes a more thorough study and
presentation of the philosophy of reconstructionism.
The ambitious scope of the new book affords clear

[24] *Ibid.*, p. 105.
[25] *Ibid.*, p. 237.

testimony of the great amount of work which must have gone into the writing of it. The work reveals the author's wide acquaintance with the educational literature of the various schools of thought at variance with his own. Most readers will be pleased, and justly so, by the way Brameld proposes to go about his task. An examination of the table of contents shows an initial section on the relationship of philosophy to education and culture. The Catholic reader, particularly, will be attracted by the consideration of ontology, epistemology and axiology. Such a beginning promises to clear the ground for an understanding discussion where we can get "behind the masks of words that divide us from one another," to use Brameld's own phrase.[26]

Following this beginning, the author gives, in appropriate sections, an exposition of each of the three philosophies which he thinks are the real rivals of reconstructionism in the field of education. The final part of the book is given over to the new philosophy. A disarming psychological approach to his readers is revealed in the opening and closing chapters of this work. They take the form of a dialogue in which a representative of each of the four schools of thought takes part in a general discussion and criticism of reconstructionism. This approach creates the atmosphere of a free and friendly discussion where everyone gets an "even break."

[26] Theodore Brameld, *Patterns of Educational Philosophy: A Democratic Interpretation* (Yonkers-on-Hudson, New York: World Book Company, 1950), p. 727.

In spite of the many merits of the book, we are forced to say that the author has not shown himself any more objective and scientific than he was in *Ends and Means in Education*. Whole sections of the earlier work are incorporated into the new exposition. Hence, the criticisms we have already made on the questions of indoctrination and authoritarianism, the supernatural and absolutes, the concept and criterion of truth, are all still valid. Other matters call for some comment.

The dramatized dialogue of the opening and closing chapters is blameworthy, not as a general method but in the way the method has been applied in this particular case. It is, of course, a very laudable attempt on the part of the author to see his own philosophy from the outside; through his speakers, indeed, he brings forward some very pertinent criticisms of reconstructionism. Naturally the author's mentality will color the objections he puts into the mouths of his characters. This is a danger and one against which Brameld does not seem to have been sufficiently on his guard.

The perennialist seems, in our eyes, to be a little unreal. He does, it is true, bring forward questions which a perennialist would likely ask of this newcomer to the philosophic horizon.[27] Yet he seems to be too easily switched from his line of thought, he does not get down to some of the fundamental points, he leaves a wrong impression of what is contained in

[27] *Ibid.*, pp. 706–720.

the essentials of his philosophy. In considering social consensus as a criterion of truth, he leads the discussion on for a certain distance and then, when he should have got to the crucial point of truth itself, he leaves the matter in mid-air. He gives the impression that only self-evident truths have a place in perennial thought. He makes no comment on social consensus as a good working arrangement for decisions on action, as perhaps a persuasive argument on the probability of a belief or truth. He does not make it clear that supernatural revelation deals with a limited, though extensive, set of truths in the perennialist theological coffer. He has nothing to say about the existence of God. Because of these deficiencies, we criticize the false atmosphere of this dialogue, the apparent free, friendly and fair discussion, which is really not so. We cannot, indeed, expect a complete presentation of the perennialist case against reconstructionism in the limits of one or two informal chapters. We know Brameld has a good deal to say, in the body of his book, on the concept of truth, the argument leading to the First Cause, and other such matters. Nevertheless, we are entitled to expect that the perennialist will, in the discussion, make the most fundamental objections from the point of view that he represents.

Brameld deserves praise for undertaking to set forth, within limits, the basic tenets of progressivism, essentialism, and perennialism. He recognizes, and we must all agree with him, that it would be impossible to treat the beliefs of each school exhaustively. He

knows that some thinkers in each school will differ as
to what they would like to see emphasized. We must
not expect from a writer who is merely clearing the
ground for his own ideas a detailed exposition of each
set of beliefs, such an exposition as would be given by
a defender of these beliefs. In these circumstances,
however, an author must remember that while he is
rightly permitted to impose limitations on his treatment, he is still bound in scientific justice not to be
unfair. It is our contention that Brameld has been unfair and unscientific in his presentation of perennialism. His global treatment, his use and non-use of
evidence, his wrong interpretations, are the testimony
to which we appeal in support of the accusation.

By his "global treatment" we mean the inclusion,
under one caption, of the philosophy of Hutchins, of
the Great Books Program and of the Catholic Church.
Differences are acknowledged but they are so inci-
dental as not to warrant a completely separate treatment for these philosophies. Is this procedure really
unscientific or does the accusation proceed from a
mind that is indoctrinated with a love for, or chained
by slavery to, one particular form of perennialism?
Lest the second question be immediately answered in
the affirmative and the matter be dismissed without
further consideration, let us recall the evidence of
Brameld's own example. He admits that reconstructionism is the offspring of progressivism and agrees
with it as far as it goes. He reveals the beliefs on which
the two schools are at one (most important among

these are the secular and materialist outlook on life, the complete rejection of absolutes and the supernatural). The differences hinge mainly on goals for the future, the complete relativism of Dewey's school, its concept of growth for more growth. In the new philosophy, thought must be goal-centered; the goals must be as concrete and precise as possible without degenerating into absolutes; social self-realization is the supreme value for the individual and social consensus is the main criterion for truth (value and truth differ only in degree). In the author's mind these differences entitle reconstructionism to consideration as a philosophy distinct and separate from, though closely allied to, progressivism. We see no reason for disagreeing with him on this point.

We are now led to examine the differences which he notices between the various kinds of perennialists.

> Particularly do differences become sharp at times between those who emphasize the religious-theological beliefs of Aquinas and those who try to keep their thought primarily secular.[28]

Brameld dislikes and rejects the supernatural—and consequently religion. He may commend some sort of secular religion, he may express an opinion that religion is too important a social force to be bandied about outside the public school by bigoted people (be it noted that to Brameld and other secularists religious

[28] *Ibid.*, pp. 293–294.

people all seem bigoted; yet people who have no use for religion are never bigoted). Brameld's religion will be religion without God, for the whole tone of his book shows that the idea of a Supreme Being is distasteful to him and regarded as superstition.[29] We disagree with the author but the only point we wish to make here is to show that his decided views on these questions reveal that he realizes the tremendous difference there must be between a philosophy that is secular and one that rests on the cornerstone of belief in God's existence and His importance in the actions of our daily life.

Hutchins believes that our problems will not be solved without religion, he believes in God, he praises the Christian virtues; yet it is not easy to find out just how deeply necessary these beliefs are to his philosophy or even what exactly those concepts of God and religion mean to him in theory and practice. In his educational scheme, on the other hand, it is clear that metaphysics is the rock on which he builds. The religious-theological beliefs of Aquinas are not, we must remember, just a supernaturalized metaphysics even though Brameld seems at times to suspect that there are no "consequential distinctions" between the ideas of Hutchins and of St. Thomas.[30] Our author sees clearly that the focus of Hutchins' thought is on metaphysics and not on religion. In the work of St. Thomas, the focus is on God. It would seem then that,

[29] *Ibid.*, p. 446.
[30] *Ibid.*, p. 336.

even for Brameld's limited purpose, a more scientific analysis of perennialism was demanded. If the differences between reconstructionism and progressivism are so great as to necessitate separation of the two philosophies, the differences between the thought of Hutchins and the philosophy of Catholic thinkers are greater and, therefore, the two schools of thought should be separated. The rebuttal of Hutchins' ideas (if such has been achieved) does not mean that the philosophy of Catholicism may be dismissed.

In the same way, the perennialism we have received from the pen of St. Thomas will suffer no severe reversal in the field of philosophy even if reconstructionism is successful in ousting the Great Books Program from the educational schemes of today. This program was certainly a departure from exaggerated vocationalism and the cult of material success. Catholics readily agree that it is a good thing for people to read books that are deservedly called great. They do not think that such reading provides education whole and complete, in so far as education can be complete. They do not agree with the choice of books as made by St. John's. And even if St. John's included or excluded books at the wish of Catholic educators, they would still probably not agree with the program as giving a sufficient education. Once again, on the relationship of this perennialism to Catholic philosophy, Brameld reveals deficient analysis. Let us quote:

> In short, the great books program is so completely in accord with perennialist beliefs about

reality, knowledge, and value in general, and about education in particular, that it would be helpful if other exponents of similar views emulated the frankness of perhaps their most profound international spokesman, Maritain. In mentioning the need to study the "heritage of philosophical wisdom," teachers, he says: "may always hope, indeed, that by virtue of its very truth, the philosophy which they think to be true, as I do Aristotelean and Thomistic philosophy, will gain momentum among their fellowmen, at least in the generation to come." [31]

There is confusion in Brameld's statement which wrongly puts on the same footing all those whom he has called perennialists. It is another example of faulty procedure. A few more quotations from this section of Maritain's argument will perhaps show where Brameld's deficiency lies.

A good philosophy should be a true philosophy. Now the professors of philosophy are bound to hold philosophical positions which differ widely. And if one of these positions is grounded on true principles, apparently the others are not. . . .[32] Now those who share in the Christian creed know that another rational wisdom, which is rooted in faith, not in reason alone, is superior to the merely human wisdom of metaphysics. . . .[33] Nobody can do without the-

[31] *Ibid.*, p. 335. Brameld quotes from J. Maritain, *Education at the Crossroads* (New Haven: Yale University Press, 1943), p. 73.
[32] Maritain, *op. cit.*, p. 72.
[33] *Ibid.*, p. 73.

ology, at least a concealed and unconscious theology, and the best way of avoiding the inconveniences of an insinuated theology is to deal with theology that is consciously aware of itself.[34]

It seems evident that Maritain did not throw himself into the camp of either Hutchins or St. John's College; he clearly states the inadequacy of metaphysics alone. Yet Brameld, although he seems aware of the differences among the various types of perennialists, so intermingles their thought in his exposition and so draws out non-existent relationships between them that his method is justly considered unscientific.

Unfortunately, at the end of this chapter [35] in which he really does show that he has given a good amount of thought and study to Catholic educational philosophers, Brameld inserts a passage that falls far below the standard we expect from a scholar of his ability and learning. The reader, if he follows the author's line, will carry away one conviction. He will be sure of the inherent wickedness of the Catholic Church and the unpatriotic activity of Catholic leaders. How scholarly, scientific, balanced and unprejudiced is a statement that appears in print in the following way?

A battery of "experts" in American history has been assembled to "prove" that the founders of the United States (James Madison, particularly) never intended that religious schools should be denied public support.[36]

[34] *Ibid.*, p. 74.
[35] Brameld, *op. cit.*, chapter XI.
[36] *Ibid.*, pp. 346–347.

In the course of his book, Brameld has spoken of educational experts; they never deserved quotation marks about their title. Hence, to a Catholic reader, the above passage is heavy with insinuation. The "experts" must be quacks, the arguments presented inane, the instigator of the whole procedure, namely, the Catholic Church, must be engaged in underhand tactics and falsification, as Brameld's readers should expect. Yet our author does not offer the names of the "experts" to give the reader a chance to judge for himself. None of the alleged proofs are given so that the reader may see for himself whether they are inane or falsified. History witnesses to the many attacks on Catholic belief and practices, attacks that appeal to prejudice. We are greatly disappointed that a man of undoubted scholarship, one who had promised the "most scrupulous inclusion and consideration of all beliefs at odds" with his own,[37] should seemingly make use of the same mode of criticism.

It is rather interesting to find that Thomas More receives attention and commendation from our author. More is recognized as the herald of modern utopianism and Brameld's philosophy is utopian.[38] This word has an invidious meaning which must be ruled out. Utopianism, as used in the explanation of reconstructionism, does not denote an attitude of mind that is merely a flight from reality; it is a "realizable vision of what could be and should be attained by man so that man would be happier, more rational, more

[37] *Ibid.*, p. 666.
[38] *Ibid.*, p. 398.

humane than he has ever been." [39] More, "the great Renaissance leader," finds himself in very strange company; he is partnered with Bellamy and H. G. Wells.[40] Strange it is, too, that Brameld never mentions that More is a canonized saint and martyr of the Catholic Church. St. Thomas More preferred to be executed rather than yield one whit on the supernaturalisms our author rejects so decisively. More chose death rather than disloyalty to that Church which seems, in the minds of Brameld and other leading educators, to be the bête noire, with communism, for all modern schemes to insure the future of democracy.

Our author is wide awake to a danger present in any argumentation; he says that sometimes "we may become aware of how readily we distort our testimony when we have no wish to do so" [41] and indeed at times we realize that our behavior is inconsistent with our beliefs. In spite of this declaration, Brameld has distorted evidence about the activity of Catholic leaders, Church authority, the Catholic idea of God, and he has failed to offer testimony for some of the charges made. We have already seen how inconsistently he applies his definition of indoctrination. Let us now consider at some length another aspect of religious schools, an aspect that forms the basis of attack for many writers.

[39] *Ibid.*, p. 397.
[40] *Ibid.*, pp. 452, 609.
[41] *Ibid.*, p. 458.

To Brameld a parochial school system, separate from the public school system, is a slur on American public schools and creates bitter divisions among the children; the same accusation is also levelled at such devices as "released time."

> Recall the profoundly hostile conceptions of reality that divide Catholic parochial schools from American public schools. . . .[42] Its [released time] most conspicuous effect is to separate children of various faiths from one another and to accentuate group differences at the very time when a culture-in-crisis needs to concern itself seriously with strengthening intergroup solidarities.[43]

It is high time that thinkers like Brameld came down to earth and reality on this topic. The Constitution of the United States, in aiming to lay the foundation for what has become the American way of life, recognizes freedom of conscience in such a way that any citizen of the United States is free to follow the religion he wants. Therefore, in so far as man can prudently foresee, there will always be different religious bodies, composed of members who have different beliefs and whose lives will be lived accordingly. With the amazing development that has placed the United States in its present high economic, national and international status, education becomes the best means for that society to guarantee each man's

[42] *Ibid.*, p. 39.
[43] *Ibid.*, p. 665.

dignity and to foster the values and promote the knowledge and character that will make a great people. Any educational system, then, that would obstruct the fulfillment of these aims is justly to be condemned, any schools which, of their nature, would set child against child, which would divide pupils in such a way as to prevent the development of a well-balanced, prosperous, democratic, American society, are not to be tolerated. In the minds of many modern thinkers, Catholic parochial schools are a glaring example of just such schools.

What are the facts of the matter? The parochial schools are divided from public schools—a perfectly obvious statement. So are the public schools of Texas or the Dakotas divided from the public schools of New York City; so are the public schools of Harlem divided from the public schools of Westchester County; so are progressive schools divided from essentialist schools; so, on the higher level, is Massachusetts State University divided from Harvard, and New York University from Columbia. The student bodies of these various schools and universities display many group differences; so also do the inhabitants of one state differ from those of another; even communities within a state may differ. Let us remember that it is people with whom we are concerned, not merely vague generalities nor even systems. It is the Americans who go into and come out from these educational institutions who should be the object of our worry. Good systems are good, good Americans are better. Perhaps the most wonderful thing about Americans is their differences; it is most wonderful because these differences exist in a oneness that makes the United States what we know them to be, a oneness that is a state of mind and a way of life. Differences in themselves are not to be condemned, they are the great merit of American democracy; only such differences as would destroy that oneness, which is a priceless treasure, should be rejected.

Religious differences, our author may assert, are in a category apart. The Constitution of the United States guarantees to the followers of the many denominations of non-Catholic religion, as well as to Catholics, Jews and others, the freedom of their religious convictions. Sectarian bigotry, Brameld may argue, is the natural offspring of religious differences and has caused strife, warfare and death among fellow Americans. True, up to a point. Religious differences do beget and have begotten bigotry; this is an unnatural, undesirable and unnecessary offspring. Sectarian bitterness has caused strife and battle, imprisonment and death. So, too, did the differences between the North and South cause a civil war, differences which are not yet wholly submerged; war should not have happened but it did. Does it really lead to dire consequences if one group of children go to one school and another group to a different one? Does the sight of one crowd of pupils going off to have religious instruction naturally incite the others against them? Do some grow up good Americans and others (at religious schools or receiving religious instruction) grow up bad citizens? Does our Catholic parochial system try to oppose the authority of the United States in favor of the authority of an "ecclesiastical elite"? Does it aim to hand over to a foreign dictator the children of American citizens? Though actual slavery has been abolished, is there now in our midst a worse type of slavery, imposed on the millions of Americans who should be good citizens but are not, because they were educated in parochial schools? Do Catholic educational leaders try to block every attempt on the part of earnest educational experts to plan for a secure democracy? An affirmative answer to these questions is expressly contained or artfully insinuated in Brameld's book.

The whole objection is ridiculous in the precise meaning of that term—laughable. Unfortunately, it is also tragic because writers like the present one take themselves seriously on this point. The testimony to support the charges is lacking. Have the parochial students grown up without imbibing the values that America treasures most? Have they proved themselves unworthy of their citizenship? Have they not contributed in a valuable way to America's democracy? Have they tried to sell out the United States to a foreign power or dictator? (Many of them had a wonderful opportunity to do so, when American troops were advancing ever closer to the "dictator" of the Vatican, during World War II.) Thus could we go through a seemingly endless list of questions. Let us content ourselves with suggesting to Brameld a few simple ways in which he might have tested, publicly and experimentally, the truth of the accusations and insinuations contained in his writing.

Thousands of non-Catholic troops, from the lowest ranks to outstanding leaders, went to the Vatican, saw the treasures of the Vatican Museum, witnessed the crowded religious services at St. Peter's. Within the small extent of Vatican City, they saw the great acclaim with which the Pope was greeted by huge crowds, the quiet reverence with which smaller groups and individuals approached him. What did these non-Catholics think? Were they witnessing the mere fawning of "sub-humans" enslaved by a dictator of the ilk of Stalin, or was it the spontaneous outburst of joy and loyalty similar to that to which some million Americans gave vent in Times Square on V-J Day, 1945? Again, with reference to the "counter-influence of superstitious and religious bigotry" [44] which makes society "so slow to apply the discoveries of science to its own welfare," [45] we would have welcomed a word or two from some Americans who are members of the Vatican Academy of Sciences; their university affiliations should remove any doubt as to whether their testimony came from clerical or Catholic bias. Such men are R. A. Millikan, physicist of California, George D. Birkhoff, mathematician of Harvard, or Taylor Hugh Scott, Princeton chemist.[46]

[44] *Ibid.*, p. 589.
[45] *Ibid.*
[46] Dorothy Fremont Grant, *Born Again* (Milwaukee: Bruce Publishing Company, 1950), p. 170.

None of this testimony was brought forth, perhaps not even investigated. Yet surely this concourse of visitors to the Vatican, non-Catholic as well as Catholic, American as well as international, set up the conditions for such a social consensus as Brameld praises in his book, a consensus not limited by national boundaries.

Perhaps another international example may help to show how unfounded are the accusations and fears of many modern educators. The Boy Scout movement is recognized as one of the best factors for the training of youth in proper values and community action. It is international and non-sectarian, it does not claim to be religious in any sense, yet is not indifferent to religion, it is a movement in which Jews, Protestants, Catholics and pagans take part. Actually, in its rules and constitutions, the Scout movement encourages members to practice their own religion more faithfully and to respect the religious beliefs of their fellow scouts. The founder refused to consider the incorporation into the Scout organization of a watered-down version or common denominator of the various religious creeds.

In a different but more concrete manner, the question of divisiveness among scouts came up in the United States. The National Committee of the Boy Scouts of America approved the conferring of religious awards. These awards were to be made, not by the National Committee, but by the religious bodies who had scouting troops. Suitable insignia

were approved for wearing on the uniform to pro-
claim the award. Then some official became uneasy.
Perhaps these badges divided, in too public a way, the
Lutheran Scout from the Catholic, the Protestant from
the Jew. After discussion, it was decided that such
religious recognition was in no way harmful or di-
visive. It is plain, of course, that any Protestant,
Jewish or Catholic child knows that his religion is different in some way from the others. He goes to a
different church on Sundays (perhaps even on week-
days), or to a synagogue on Saturdays. Whether he is
in public school or not, he is well aware of these differences. They arise in real-life situations and, after
all, the school is supposed to be as real-life as possible.
But there is no harm in this awareness of differences,
even to a "culture-in-crisis." We submit, however, one
warning. There will be divisiveness when pupils and
teachers are led to despise those of a different religion,
to regard them with suspicion, to believe that they
are un-American, that they do not value freedom and
are not permitted to and cannot think for themselves.
Nowhere are these attitudes and beliefs proposed to
teachers, to working people, to parents, and hence to
pupils, more clearly than in works like Brameld's
Patterns of Educational Philosophy.

Is it possible that we have given too much attention
to our author's mentality and ideas on religion? He
regards it as important, though for him this importance seems negative rather than positive. He tells us
that it is too important a social factor to be left to

"doctrinaire treatment outside public education." [47] From what he has done in his writing, we gather that it is perfectly legitimate to give religion doctrinaire treatment inside public education, inside the exposition of reconstructionism. As long as this doctrinaire treatment comes from those who condemn religion, everything is permissible.

Brameld tells us that it is "now imperative that we know as clearly as we can where we want to go . . ."[48] as the vision of great human possibilities crystallizes into clear-cut plausible goals." [49] We can, it may be, form some idea of the confidence we should have in this type of educational expert, from the following quotation—a good example of the use of words to cloak thought.

> Perhaps the most important aim is to reconsider religious values. Utilizing their own earlier study of religion in the human relations area, students now seek to view this elusive but important goal-seeking interest in the perspective of all areas of study. Free play of the esthetic imagination, including its unrational qualities, is especially wanted here. If motivation is successful, the meaning of the "cultural myth" deepens. Parts of the design blend together like colors of the spectrum. And students come to appreciate more intimately, more poignantly, that life can be meaningful, exciting, purposeful for anyone who feels himself in some way part of the age-

[47] Brameld, *op. cit.*, p. 667.
[48] *Ibid.*, p. 440.
[49] *Ibid.*, p. 455.

old quest for earth-wide satisfaction of the supreme goals of humanity.[50]

By "unrational" Brameld means all those powers that are not rational in the individual's social life [51]—a very enlightening definition. Yet, let the Catholic Church introduce the esthetic into its rituals, its vestments, its music, its ceremonies, its symbols—let Catholic philosophers speak of man's rational powers and his physical powers and they are condemned for introducing superstition, for postulating a dichotomy in man's nature, separating the mind from the body. The "age-old" seeking after the supreme goals of humanity is, according to reconstructionism, the "maximum satisfaction of the maximum wants to the maximum number of human beings." [52] We must not, however, lose sight of the criterion for that "maximum." Brameld is willing to apply social consensus as criterion of those maximum wants, though he recognizes its limitations, in that it "turns out to be too often the consensus of a *part* of some social group—a part able to dominate the remainder because it controls the instruments of power and propaganda, or perhaps because the others are too indifferent or ignorant to care." [53] In other words, the values, the supreme goals are likely to be determined by a minority, or by the fifty-one per

[50] *Ibid.*, p. 608.
[51] *Ibid.*, p. 447.
[52] *Ibid.*, p. 583.
[53] *Ibid.*, p. 462.

cent. These goals, determined by social consensus, are the goals Brameld sets before human society; he rejects any supernatural aim in life, as we well know, any life after death; he disagrees with what has been traditionally sought as the supreme goal of life. We disagree with him on these points; we do not argue with him. We do, however, argue against his applying the designation of "age-old" to the quest that has been featured by such writers as himself only from the time that religion was ousted as an important social factor in public life. Brameld has no great respect for the age-old quest nor for age-old goals; he has respect for the goals of modern reconstructionism. Why cause confusion by seeming to agree with what man has always sought, namely, religious values? The reconsideration our author wants to give to religious values is rejection, not reconsideration. Here, indeed, we have an instance of "the masks of words" that tend to deceive, even though the author himself may be sincere.

Since goal-seeking is the most important aspect in which reconstructionism differs from its parent progressivism, it would be well to know what goals mean to this new school of thought. The focus of the new philosophy is on the future. We know what the future could be like and therefore should be like, and will be like if we take decisive action.[54] The goals to be aimed at must be grasped as clearly as possible.[55] This is a

[54] *Ibid.*, p. 435.
[55] *Ibid.*, p. 440.

welcome departure from the vagueness of the Dewey school, but it seems to be sailing perilously close to the winds of absolutism—a horrible disaster for a reconstructionist. Progressivism was afraid to speak of a planned society, whereas Brameld has no bias against a blue-print for the future, meaning thereby "deliberate, systematic, organized constructions of future cultural objectives." [56] It is important to "keep such goals always integral with the dominant national and international purposes of our times." [57] We may have here nothing more than a sound democratic principle; there is danger, however, that it spells servitude to expedient politics of a particular regime which happens to determine the dominant policies of a particular time. Brameld himself, we well know, does not wish for such servitude because he rules out ward-heel politics when he claims that the school should be the co-partner of politics in a democracy.[58] But we cannot accept reconstructionism merely because of the author's sincerity; even his own criterion of social consensus demands more.

The author has admitted that his social consensus may be no more than the wishes of a powerful but small group. This small minority or bare majority may have offensive policies legally authorized. Such policies seem to be among Brameld's guides to morality.

[56] *Ibid.*, p. 497.
[57] *Ibid.*, p. 539.
[58] *Ibid.*, p. 756.

> . . . means that violate policies legally author-
> ized by the majority are immoral means.[59]

It is true that this basic principle of Brameld's teaching speaks of a majority. In point of fact, it is the
people's representatives who finally determine the
policies; the majority that carried the decision may
have been small or was perhaps unduly influenced. In
spite of this possibility and its consequences, these
policies are to become guides to morality, showing
thus that reconstructionist morality is merely legal.
We do not advocate disobedience to laws before they
have been removed from the statute book, but we do
object to the "maneuvers of minorities who benefit
by the indifference of majorities" [60] becoming our
ultimate standard of moral values. Brameld also seems
to introduce again in new guise that authoritarianism
which he condemned so forcefully; the "dominant
purposes demanded by our age" seem to wield such
an influence on the elementary school.

> Once these purposes are clear, the elementary
> school is endowed with a direction that governs
> every step of the way. . . .[61]

A very noteworthy omission in Brameld's treatise is
the bypassing of the truth of God's existence. The
author rejects all supernaturalisms and he holds for a
complete secularism. According to the scientific

[59] *Ibid.*, p. 605.
[60] *Ibid.*, p. 719.
[61] *Ibid.*, p. 612.

method as he accepts it, our author is responsible for proving that God does not exist; without this proof, we cannot even begin to consider his philosophy. It is not sufficient for him to assert that there is no supernatural; it is not sufficient to make passing insinuations that the acceptance of a Supreme Being to whom we are responsible for our actions is a relic of superstition or the effect of ecclesiastic authoritarianism. If we apply Brameld's criterion, social consensus, to this truth, we find that for more centuries than secularism has been accepted, belief in God was accepted. Anthropological or ethnological investigations reveal that belief in a Supreme Being is universally upheld even among remote nations, tribes and civilizations of the world. We do not need to deny that superstition sometimes colors this belief. Our author's criterion is artfully left to one side when it tells against his own theories.

Many other matters we might bring forward to indicate the writer's authoritarian definitions, his misrepresentation of Catholic perennial beliefs, his unscientific treatment and his prejudice. They would take us far beyond the scope of this book. We think there is enough evidence in the foregoing pages to reveal in Brameld's method, knowledge and interpretation, sufficiently serious faults to cast doubts on his role as an educational expert, devoted to scientific and intellectual fair play in disposing of the arguments of those whose beliefs are at variance with his own.

Chapter Six . . . DEMOCRATIC APPLICATION OF SCIENTIFIC METHOD

The study we have pursued in the foregoing chapters has been negative. The reader will look in vain for an orderly explanation of Catholic philosophy. He will fail to find a deep philosophic presentation of any Catholic tenets mentioned in the book. He will, we hope, find one thing which this work aimed at revealing. He will find that the Catholic stand in the educational field has not been considered, has been unfairly treated, or has been completely misrepresented.

On the other hand, he will have met but little commendation of what is good in the experimentalist theory of education. He will have seen but a small measure of constructive consideration of the philosophy defended by the men whose writings we have studied. We have not failed our reader for we promised him none of these things. He must look elsewhere for them. Works which give an exposition of our philosophy or present our philosophic rejection of the basic beliefs of experimentalism are much weightier and more valuable than this. But if road-blocks are erected and inscribed with the sign: KEEP OUT, at every intersection and crossroads where the signposts point to Catholic education or to Catholic philosophy, how can the sincere reader possibly know by experimental procedure what lies along these roads? This essay is an invitation to the passer-by to push aside the road-blocks and see for himself.

Since most of the books we examined were expositions of progressive philosophy, a certain uniform pattern has run through the material we have considered. Indeed, we could have found in almost any one of the authors all the points on which we have based our criticism. That, however, would not have served our purpose. There is sufficient freedom and respect for individuality in any school of thought for each follower to be responsible for his own shortcomings. Thus the deficiencies in scientific method and understanding which we would have disclosed by concentrating on one author could have been attributed to the scientific and philosophical limitations of that individual. In presenting the number of outstanding progressive thinkers who have appeared on these pages, we have given clear evidence that their deficiencies are not idiosyncrasies but part and parcel of the particular school of educational philosophy.

There was a danger in this style of treatment, a danger that we tried to avoid. Since the same ideas of Catholic belief were presented in most of the writings, the same distorted interpretations, the same accusations and the same lack of due consideration, there was the possibility of each chapter being but a duplicate of the preceding. Progressive writers are steeped in each other's thought—a sign of the close cohesion of Dewey's followers. To read one presentation of their philosophy is to be already acquainted with most of the matter that another spokesman will offer, though there will, of course, be different emphases. Our method of avoiding an overpowering monotony was to refrain from treating in more than a cursory way in one author what was given extended attention in another. This does not imply that each one is guilty only of the major deficiencies we emphasized in his particular case. It was, of course, impossible to avoid completely a repetition of criticism. Hence, it will have become evident that there are a number of concepts on which we are at complete variance with the progressives, there are misrepresentations of Catholic ideas that occur with unfailing regularity, there are unfounded accusations against the Church that appear continually.

The reader himself will have no difficulty in detecting this pattern. There is no need to do more than pass in review the main themes which were called on parade in the pages of our criticism. They centered around such concepts as man and his nature, God and His existence and practical bearing on everyday life; the Church and authoritarianism, totalitarianism and science; the nature of democracy, morality and religion; the foundations and aims of social life; the role of the material and spiritual; the educational implications of such notions; the nature and scope of education in modern scientific society.

While such ideas as we have reviewed would immediately strike the reader as having a very important place in this study, with their progressive counterparts assuming a major role in that philosophy, several important threads of thought in the experimental school may have escaped his notice. Progressive writers present as interesting and accurate a picture of modern society as one could wish for. They see the world about them, the family, the school, the state, nations and peoples, in all of which the individual person is the important factor. They see that, like it or not, the peoples of the earth have now reached a stage of internationalism; national boundaries no longer confine the influences of policies, values, and conduct. All of this can be revealed accurately by a good reporter, using the term in its best sense. It is factual; it is not a matter of interpretation. Each school of thought will offer its own interpretation.

In the intellectual field a similar transcending of limits and boundaries has taken place; this phenomenon makes itself recognizable in any specific presentation of the experimental educational philosophy. We are aware that the extent of knowledge and science has so expanded that no one can be master of all the sciences, perhaps not even of all the branches of one science. Centuries ago, the outstanding leaders of thought were experts in many fields. Today, however, that is almost impossible; hence, the need for specialization. It is easy for the investigator to reach this conclusion. The converse to it is the phenomenon to which we wish to draw attention. Many of the sciences, particularly outside what are known as the exact sciences, can no longer be strictly limited. Education is one such science.

Let us make the matter clearer. Most of the books we have chosen for our study are expositions of educational philosophy. Yet the sociologist could examine them with profit and believe that they were in great part sociological studies. The expert in political science would find much material from his sphere; the apostles of religion will discover a great deal about morality; the professional exponent of general philosophy will see his pet concepts bandied about, explicitly and implicitly. Economics, labor-management relations, business, even party politics, will find a share of attention. What, then, is this philosophy of education which seems to have no bounds? Has this science the right to probe into so many specialized fields as it undoubtedly does?

Far be it from us to suggest that such probing is a fault, much less a subject on which to criticize the progressive school of thought. It is, rather, a virtue; educational philosophy must interest itself in these fields. Otherwise, it will fail to keep in touch with reality, and hence will fail to educate. But we have a fault to find. Why do the progressive philosophers think that educators (especially progressive educators) are the experts best fitted to lead all the rest, best fitted to tell them how to save democracy, best fitted to teach them the sacredness of the individual? This attitude is in reality a manifestation under a new name of the authoritarianism they so loudly reject.

We are not surprised that the followers of this school do pay homage to authority nor are we surprised at the importance given to the role of the educational expert in particular. An expert is one who, through deep study, keen observation, long and varied experience, acquires a comprehensive and practical knowledge of his particular field. There are leaders to whom the experimental thinkers would grant such a distinction. John Dewey is an obvious example. Many of his followers have regarded him as the greatest philosopher of this twentieth century and have accepted his statements on educational matters just because he made them. Such is the authority of the expert. It is an authority worthy to be accepted when the expert is truly such, deep in knowledge, wide in experience, balanced in judgment and prudent in practice.

Human nature does not change quickly in its values nor in its externals. Even if we, like the progressives, gave allegiance to Darwinian evolution, we would find our estimation of the time needed for evolutions based not on periods of five or ten years, nor yet on fifty nor hundred year cycles. In the Darwinian calendar, tens of thousands of years may be common parlance. To be practical, however, we are interested in our Western culture as it has developed up to the present time; we are interested in the future, especially in the immediate future. To go back to the roots of Western culture will not bring us beyond the span of a few thousand years. It is true that science has made great changes in civilization, especially in the last few hundred years. It is true, also, that during these few thousand years man has not fundamentally changed, though his surroundings have. The Catholic Church has guided men, has educated them, has tried to bring them a measure of happiness. At some periods her success has been greater than at others; at times, her guidance has been rejected wholly or in part. Success she has had and will have. She has behind her the experience of twenty centuries; she has dealt with men in their most intimate ideals and difficulties; she has studied human nature from all angles; she has recognized men's needs and hopes; she has watched empires, kingdoms, nations rise and fall; she has suffered persecutions of the greatest intensity; she has built up a Christian civilization in which American democracy, as any other, must find its roots. These truths are not a matter of divine revelation; they are not accepted on blind authority; they are material from the open pages of history. Yet, because a group of educators, knowingly or in good faith, have for the last fifty years engaged in a continual campaign of misrepresentation, misunderstanding and vilification, American Catholics are expected to stand by in meek submission and see themselves branded as slaves, deceivers, and traitors. They are expected to agree, with abject consent, when progressive intellectuals condemn the beliefs they cherish, despise the religion they love, and push to one side the God whom they and many other Americans still worship.

It is true that the indictment we have brought against the scholarship and fairness of these progressive educators applies only to a limited aspect of their writings. But this aspect, namely, their treatment of the Catholic Church and of Catholic philosophy, can on no account be considered insignificant or unworthy of careful and considerate handling. About one-fifth of the American people are Catholics; Catholic schools are the outstanding example of free enterprise in education and they educate annually more Americans than were in all thirteen colonies at the time of the Revolution; hundreds of times more people the world over—scholars and non-scholars—subscribe to Catholic theology and philosophy than subscribe to the recently formulated theories of progressives; twenty centuries of intellectual criticism and refinement undergird today's Catholic philosophy of education. In all of these respects—in numbers, in educational activity, in wide acceptance of Catholic thought, and in honorable tradition—the educational teaching and policies of the Catholic Church should receive extensive and scientifically critical attention from contemporary non-Catholic educators. Yet we have seen how these leaders of American educational thought dismiss Catholic ideas regarding life and education by using catchwords, insinuations, prejudgments, and unsubstantiated charges. There is little evidence either of honest investigation or even of a sincere desire to achieve objectivity whenever the Catholic Church enters their writing.

Progressive educators have been loud in their defense of academic freedom—freedom to teach and freedom to learn. In so far as we can generalize from these undoubted leaders of contemporary education, we wonder what freedom of learning there is for students in the teachers' colleges and schools of education across the country in discussion of the Catholic Church and her theory of education.

If defense were needed for undertaking a study such as this, we could do no better than quote from one of the books criticized in Chapter I. John Dewey and John L. Childs are the authors of the chapter in *The Educational Frontier* in which the following words appear as a footnote.

> Criticism of the philosophy we advance [i.e., progressivism] is likely, therefore, to be effective as it centers upon, first, the criteria we employ, and, second, the correctness and adequacy of the use we have made of them in interpreting and recording the social situation in which we live.[1]

It is for the reader to determine whether, by these standards, our criticism has been effective.

[1] Kilpatrick, ed., *The Educational Frontier*, p. 294.

BIBLIOGRAPHY

AQUINAS, St. Thomas, *Summa Theologica*.

BODE, Boyd H., *Modern Educational Theories*. New York: The Macmillan Company, 1927.

————, *Progressive Education at the Crossroads*. New York: Newson and Company, 1938.

————, *Democracy as a Way of Life*. New York: The Macmillan Company, 1948.

BRAMELD, Theodore, *Ends and Means in Education: A Midcentury Appraisal*. First edition; New York: Harper and Brothers, 1950.

————, *Patterns of Educational Philosophy: A Democratic Interpretation*. Yonkers-on-Hudson, New York: World Book Company, 1950.

CHILDS, John L., *Education and the Philosophy of Experimentalism*. New York: Appleton-Century-Crofts, Inc., 1931.

————, *Education and Morals: An Experimental Philosophy of Education*. New York: Appleton-Century-Crofts, Inc., 1950.

GILLIN, John Lewis, *Criminology and Penology*. Third edition; New York: D. Appleton-Century Company, 1945.

GRANT, Dorothy Fremont, *Born Again*. Milwaukee: Bruce Publishing Company, 1950.

HEALY, William and Bronner, Augustine, *New Light on Delinquency and its Treatment: Results of a Research Conducted for the Institute of Human Relations, Yale University*. New Haven: Yale University Press, 1936.

HOOK, Sidney, *Education for Modern Man*. New York: The Dial Press, 1946.

159

KALLEN, Horace M., *The Education of Free Men: An Essay Toward a Philosophy of Education for Americans*. New York: Farrar, Straus and Young, Inc., 1949.

KILPATRICK, William Heard, *Education for a Changing Civilization*. New York: The Macmillan Company, 1927.

————, editor, *The Educational Frontier*. New York: Appleton-Century-Crofts, Inc., 1933.

MARITAIN, JACQUES, *Education at the Crossroads*. New Haven: Yale University Press, 1949.

MURRAY, Raymond W. and Flynn, Frank T., *Social Problems*. New York: F. S. Crofts & Co., 1947.

PIUS XI, *The Catholic Priesthood: An Encyclical Letter*. Washington, D. C.: National Catholic Welfare Conference, 1936.

QUILLER-COUCH, Sir Arthur, *On the Art of Writing*. New York: G. P. Putnam's Sons, 1916.

RAUP, R. Bruce, Axtelle, George E., Benne, Kenneth D., Smith, B. Othanel, *The Improvement of Practical Intelligence: The Central Task of Education*. New York: Harper and Brothers, 1950.

RECKLESS, Walter C., and Smith, Mapheus, *Juvenile Delinquency*. New York: McGraw-Hill Book Co., Inc., 1932.

RIESEL, Victor and Levenstein, Aaron, "Labor Priests," *Look Magazine*, XIII, March 1, 1949, 35–39.

SHEEHAN, Most Rev. M., *Apologetics and Catholic Doctrine*. Dublin: M. H. Gill & Son, Ltd., 1942.

————, *The Pope and the People: Select Letters and Addresses on Social Questions*. London: Catholic Truth Society, 1903.

TREACY, Rev. Gerald C., editor, *Five Great Encyclicals*. New York: The Paulist Press, 1948.

INDEX

Absolutes, 37, 38, 43, 53
Academic freedom. *See* Teaching, freedom of
Adler, Mortimer, 94
Apriorism, 12
Aristotle, 18, 41, 106
  on change, 14, 17
Authoritarianism, 26, 28
  definition, 11
  in public education, 121
  supernatural, 26
Authority, 11, 67
  external, 11, 13–14
  internal, 11, 14
Behaviorism (Psychology) 60
Belief and doubt, philosophy of, 15
Bellamy, Edward, 136
Birkhoff, George D., 141
Bode, Boyd H., 29–53
  on absolutes, 36
  on democracy, 34–35
  on indoctrination, 48–49
  on traditional education, 22
  teaching of, 45–53
Boy Scout movement, 142–143
Brameld, Theodore, 114–149
  Ends and Means in Education, 127
  Patterns of Educational Philosophy, 125–149
Capital, 39
Carrel, Alexis, 96
Catholic Church, claims of, 116
  educational teaching, 2–3, 156–157
  quoted on parochial schools, 70

Catholicism. *See* Catholicity
Catholicity, 5–6
Change, 9, 14–18, 20, 53
Child labor, 111–112
Child Labor Amendment, 111–112
Childs, John L., 24, 54–82
  Education and Morals: An Experimental Philosophy of Education, 70
  on authoritarianism in education, 80–81
  on authority, 67
  on education, 62–63
  on fixed standards, 65–67
  on ideas, 64
  on individuality, 61–64
  on morality, 77
  on parochial schools, 70, 72–76
  on personality, 75
Church schools, 72–74, 108, 137–142
  Childs on, 75–76
Columbia University. Teachers College, 9, 54
Communism, 39
Conduct of life, principles of, 33
Constitution of the U. S. *See* U. S. Constitution
Crime. *See* Crime and criminals
Crime and criminals, and religious education, 101–103
Darwin, Charles Robert, 15
Declaration of Independence. *See* U. S. Declaration of Independence

161

INDEX

Democracy, 1–2, 10, 30–36, 38
Dewey, John, 2–3, 9, 24, 29, 92, 155
Dictatorship, definition, 38
Divine revelation. *See* Revelation, Divine
Dogma, 45
Doubt. *See* Belief and doubt
Dualism, 59
Education
  and morals, 82
  and religion, 20
  Catholic, 41–46
  Childs' ideas on, 62–63
  democratic, 30
  experimental methods, 2, 5, 28, 54–91
    philosophy of, 4–5
    techniques, 3–4
  right of parents, 42
  standards, 65–67
  traditional, 22
    authoritarianism in, 80–81
Essentialism (education), 118
Ethics, 89–90
  Childs on, 77
Experimentalism. *See* Education, experimental methods
Expert, definition, 155
Fabre, Jean Henri, 96
Gettysburg Address, 27
Goal seeking, human, Brameld on, 144–149
God, belief in, 148–149
Great Books Program, 129, 132. *See also* St. John's College, Annapolis, Great Books Program
Hitler, Adolf, 106
Hook, Sidney, 92–103
  Education for Modern Man, quoted, 93

Hoover, J. Edgar, 2
  and juvenile delinquency, 102–103
Hutchins, Robert M., 40–43, 94, 118
  on religion and metaphysics, 131–132
Individual, rights of, 1, 98
Individuality, 23
  Childs on, 61–64
Indoctrination, 93
  Brameld on, 119–123
Industrial relations, 78–79
Industrialism, 10
Infallibility, papal. *See* Popes, infallibility
Intelligence, 55
  definition, 59
Justice, 34
  intellectual, 1–8
Juvenile delinquency, and religious education, 101–103
Kallen, Horace, 103–113
  criticism of Catholic education, 105–111
  philosophy of education, 104–107
Kilpatrick, William Heard, 9–28
  The Educational Frontier, 22, 25
    quoted on progressivism, 158
Labor, 39
Labor relations. *See* Industrial relations
Lag, social, 16
Law, natural. *See* Natural law
Learning, definition, 19
Leo XIII, Pope, *The Condition of the Working Classes,* 111

Leo XIII, Pope (*Cont.*):
Immortale Dei, quoted, 110
on private property, 78
on the state, 113
Life, way of, 69
Lincoln, Abraham, mentioned, 27
Lippmann, Walter, 65
Man, common, 33
rights, 33, 34–39
Maritain, Jacques, 94
quoted on metaphysics, 132–134
Metaphysics, 94
Millikan, Robert Andrews, 141
Morality. *See* Ethics
More, Thomas, St., 136
and Utopianism, 135–136
Mussolini, Benito, 106
National Committee of the Boy Scouts of America, 142
National Society of College Teachers of Education, 21
Natural law, 89
Nature, human. *See* Man
New York University, 114
Obscurantism, 23
Ohio. State University, 29
Oregon School Case, decision cited, 72
Parochial schools. *See* Church schools
Pasteur, Louis, 96
Perennialism, 118, 123–125
Personality, Childs on, 75
Philosophy, experimental, 61
Pius XI, Pope, *Letter on the Christian Education of Youth,* 109
on priesthood, 51
on the state, 113

Pius XI, Pope (*Cont.*):
quoted on Church's rights in education, 71
Plato, 106
Popes, infallibility, 110
Pragmatism, 2
Prejudice, 92–113
Progressivism, 2, 9–28, 31–32, 118
Reconstructionism, 114–149
and progressivism, 114, 129–130, 146
Relativism, 29–53
Released time, 105, 137
Religion, and science, 97
Brameld on, 130–131
freedom of, 139–143
Hutchins on, 130–131
teaching of, 97–101
Revelation, Divine, 24
Rutgers University, New Brunswick, N.J., 9
Ryan, John, Msgr., 111
St. John's College, Annapolis, Great Books Program, 132, 134
Schools, sectarian, 57–58
Scientific Method, 82–84
application of, 150–158
Scott, Taylor Hugh, 141
Sex instruction, 42
Sheen, Fulton, Bp., 94
Slavery, institution of, cited, 16
Social lag. *See* Lag, social
Society, American, development of, 69
Soul
and body, relationship, 94–95
immortal, 96
Stalin, Joseph V., 106
Standards, fixed. *See* Education, standards

State, authority, 39
Symbolism, value of, 85–86
Teachers College. *See* Columbia University. Teachers College
Teaching, freedom of, 158
Thomas Aquinas, St., 41, 93, 106
  quoted on private property, 77–78
Thomists, 92, 94
Thought and thinking, progressive, 25
Tradition, 12, 36

Truth
  absolute, 35–36
  tested, 11, 12
U. S. Constitution, 31, 35
U. S. Declaration of Independence, 31
Utopias, definition, 135–136
Utopianism. *See* Utopias
Vatican Academy of Sciences, 141
Warfare, class, 39
Wells, H. G., 136
Words, psychological effect of, 86–88

A NOTE ON THE TYPE
IN WHICH THIS BOOK IS SET

This book is set in Janson, a Linotype face, created from the early punches of Anton Janson, who settled in Leipzig around 1670. This type is not an historic revival, but rather a letter of fine ancestry, remodelled and brought up to date to satisfy present-day taste. It carries a feeling of being quite compact and sturdy. It has good color and displays a pleasing proportion of ascenders and descenders as compared to the height of the lower case letters. The book was composed and printed by the York Composition Company, Inc., of York, Pa., and bound by Moore and Company of Baltimore. The typography and design are by Howard N. King.